PL
984
.E3   The Silence of love
S5
Cop. 1

DATE			

The Silence of Love

PUBLISHED WITH THE SUPPORT OF
THE MAURICE J. SULLIVAN & FAMILY FUND
IN THE UNIVERSITY OF HAWAII FOUNDATION

The Silence of Love

TWENTIETH-CENTURY KOREAN POETRY

Edited and with an Introduction
by Peter H. Lee

THE UNIVERSITY PRESS OF HAWAII • HONOLULU

Library of Congress Cataloging in Publication Data

Main entry under title:

The Silence of love.

  Bibliography: p.
  Includes index.
  1. Korean poetry—20th century—Translations into
English. 2. English poetry—20th century—Translation
from Korean. I. Lee, Peter H., 1929–
PL984.E3S5   895.7'1308   80–21999
ISBN 0-8248-0711-1
ISBN 0-8248-0732-4 (pbk.)

for Josephine Miles and Leonard Nathan

Contents

Acknowledgments

In June 1977 I asked the opinion of my colleagues regarding the contents of this anthology. With their suggestions and upon independent consultation with poets and critics in Korea, I compiled a list of poets which was approved in September 1977 by the translators, who circulated their works for reading in advance in April 1978. With the support of the Joint Committee on Korean Studies of the American Council of Learned Societies and the Social Science Research Council, we met in June 1978 at the University of Washington in Seattle to discuss the translations.

Judgments will vary, but we think that the development of modern Korean poetry can best be traced through the works of these sixteen poets who are likely to occupy a permanent place in the Korean poetic tradition. To demonstrate the originality and variety of modern Korean poetry, each poet is represented by a substantial selection, arranged chronologically, giving some impression of his development, his persistent concerns, and the world he inhabits. Biographical data and other information provided in the headnotes will help the reader to place the poets in their contexts.

I wish to express my thanks to the Joint Committee on Korean Studies for their support of the project; to the poets and their heirs for their permission to translate the poems and for answering my questions; and to Stuart Kiang and Rob Wilson for their helpful suggestions.

Finally, I wish to acknowledge with thanks permission to reprint copyrighted material:

Earle M. Coleman Enterprises, Inc., Publishers, for Kim Chi-ha's "No One," "By the Sea," "Two A.M.," "Yellow Earth Road," "January 1974," "A Smile," and "Story of a Sound," from *The Middle Hour,* translated by David R. McCann. © 1980 by Earle M. Coleman Enterprises, Inc.

George Allen & Unwin and The University Press of Hawaii, for Yi Yuksa's "The Lake," "The Summit," and "Deep-Purple Grapes"; Yun Tong-ju's "Self-Portrait"; and Pak Tu-jin's "Peaches Are in Bloom," from *Poems from Korea* (1974).

International Poetry Review, for Sŏ Chŏng-ju's "Alleyway," "The Bride," "Beside a Chrysanthemum," and "Poem of Sudaedong," translated by David R. McCann.

Modern Poetry in Translation, for Sŏ Chŏng-ju's "The Huge Wave," "Old-fashioned Hours," "Rhododendron," "Snow Days," and "Winter Sky," translated by David R. McCann.

Paul Elek Limited, for Pak Tu-jin's "A Message from the Crane" and "April"; Pak

Mogwŏl's "Untitled" and "A Meteorite"; and Shin Kyŏng-nim's "Today," from *The Elek Book of Oriental Verse,* edited by Keith Bosley and published by Paul Elek Ltd. (London, 1979) and John Weatherhill, Inc. (New York and Tokyo, 1979). © 1979 by Keith Bosley and Paul Elek Ltd.

PEN American Center, for Shin Kyŏng-nim's "Country Bus Station" and "Market's Closing," translated by David R. McCann.

Sammy E. Solberg, for selections from Han Yong-un. © 1971 by S. E. Solberg.

Translation, for Shin Kyŏng-nim's "That Day," translated by David R. McCann.

Introduction

The advent in Korea of a poetry that can be considered essentially modern in spirit was preceded by a transitional period, the period of songs and new poetry during the last decade of the nineteenth and the first decade of the present century.

The opening of Korean ports in 1876 prompted the spread of songs *(ch'angga)* to warn the people of the danger of foreigners and to bring out the need of enlightenment and reform. After the Second Japanese-Korean Convention of 1905, which made Korea Japan's protectorate, contemporary newspapers carried the songs, most of them denouncing government corruption and stressing the urgency of national independence, public enlightenment, and patriotic fervor. The song writers who produced the *ch'angga* still used traditional verse forms such as the *sijo* and *kasa,* or the song form, whose predominant pattern was 7 and 5 syllables. They were beginning to grope for a new verse form, but did not successfully break away from the limits of the traditional prosody, the prescribed alternation of 4's and 3's, and the use of traditional forms of speech and allusion.

The "new poetry" movement is usually traced back to the publication in 1908 of "From the Sea to Children" by Ch'oe Namsŏn (1890–1957), in *Sonyŏn* (Children), the first literary journal launched to initiate cultural reform by educating the masses in the new civilization of the West. The speaker in the poem is the sea, and it addresses its call to those bearing the hopes of a new generation. Inspired by Byron's *Childe Harold's Pilgrimage,* Ch'oe celebrates in clean, masculine diction the power of the young, as beacons in the darkness, who will carry out a necessary social and literary revolution.

Ch'oe experimented with a variety of traditional and hybrid verse forms—songs, "new poetry," free verse, and the *sijo.* But like earlier song writers, an orator in poet's clothing, Ch'oe was primarily concerned with the introduction of Western learning and the arousing of national consciousness. From quarrels with others he made rhetoric—slogan, propaganda, pamphlet. He and others like him were intent on action, but could not convert action into thought nor make poems out of social and political realities. He seldom spoke in his own voice. He witnessed the death of old structures, but could not erect a new edifice of form to replace them.

In 1919, shortly before the unsuccessful and costly movement for Korean independence of the same year, a powerful Western influence on Korean poetry began to appear in Korean literary journals, through translations from Verlaine, Gourmont, and Fyodor Sologub. The tenets of French Symbolism, the art of indirection and magical suggestiveness, were introduced by Kim Ŏk (1895–?), the principal translator. Against the didacticism of the age Kim invoked Mallarmé —"To name an object is to suppress three-fourths of the delight of the poem which is derived from the pleasure of divining little by little: to *suggest* it, that is the dream." And against rhetoric and sentimentality, Verlaine: "Car nous voulons la Nuance encor, / Pas la Couleur, rien que la nuance!" To Kim, Rimbaud's "Les Voyelles" was the supreme example of musical verse in Symbolist technique and a line from Baudelaire's "Correspondances"—"Les parfums, les couleurs et les sons se répondent"—the ultimate in modern poetry; but he himself failed in his own work to see correspondences between the material world and spiritual realities and those between the different human senses. He concluded that *vers libre* was the supreme creation of the Symbolists, but ignored Baudelaire's aspiration toward mysticism, that "almost Wordsworthian quest for 'spots of time,'" and the use of art as another cosmos which transforms and humanizes nature.

Kim Ŏk and other translators active in the late 1910s and early '20s reacted against sentimentality, rhetoric, descriptiveness, didacticism, and political and public themes, and attempted to mingle sound and symbol to create a strange beauty in their works. Kim's absorption with Symbolism culminated in March 1921 with the publication of *Dance of Anguish (Onoe ŭi mudo)*, the first volume of translations from Western poetry. It included Verlaine, Gourmont, Samain, Baudelaire, Yeats, and others, a total of eighty-five poems. Like Ueda Bin's *Sound of the Tide (Kaichōon,* 1905) and Nagai Kafū's *Corals (Sangoshū,* 1913), the book was at once acclaimed as beautiful translation into the native language, and it became the favorite reading of aspiring poets till the '40s. Translating from the Japanese, English, French, and Esperanto, Kim produced a mellifluous, soft, dreamy language, often using the effect of colloquial honorific verb endings. The exotic, the strange and sad beauty of autumn, ennui, anguish—all this appealed to poets who sought models for their frustration, emptiness, and feeling of despair after the collapse of the Independence Movement of 1919. This, together with Kim's first volume of new verse (1923), made known the heritage of Symbolism and advanced the development of modern Korean poetry.

At about the same time, Tagore, through the translation of *Gitanjali* (1923) and other works, became an informing spirit suited to the temper of the age. Known in Korea mainly as a prophet for a people suffering under Japanese colonial rule, and as the voice of freedom and independence, Tagore was read for his call to patriotic self-sacrifice and his belief in poetry as the vital expression of life. Tagore's subject matter, diction, tone, and poetic devices inspired a number of poets, including Han Yong-un and Kim Sowŏl.

Han Yong-un (1879–1944), one of the great poets of modern Korea, was a man of many gifts: he was a revolutionary, reformer, monk, poet, and prophet. To Han and later poets of resistance, the loss of country was an omnipresent condition of consciousness. Han sought to bring enlightenment to the terrible fate of self and country, and found the most adequate lyric form in Buddhist contemplative poetry. In 1926 he published *The Silence of Love,* comprising eighty-eight meditative poems. Wishing to address great issues, he rediscovered the symbolic Korean word *nim* (love and the beloved; also king, god, country, Buddha, etc.) to correspond to his perceptions and embody his vision. By coming back to a single word of manifold dimensions, he successfully communicated the whole measure of his personal anxieties, questionings, and final illumination. His imagery is at once simple, startling, and paradoxical—evocative of deep mysteries rooted in the mind. Han's "lamp," for example, may be the lamp that awaits the rebirth of the fatherland or that burns brightly in his consciousness upon attaining the reality of relativity. The beloved who experiences this relativity has experienced Emptiness *as* Emptiness, and glimpsed the unsurpassed wisdom or perfect enlightenment of the Buddha, the true form *(tathatā)* of Emptiness. But despite Han's (and our) longing for reunion, the *nim,* who is truly nonexistent but mysteriously existent, has not returned.

Kim Sowŏl (1902–1934) is another poet who explores the expanded meanings of the word *nim* and others of like dimension. As a poet of nature and folk tradition, Kim depends for his effectiveness on the simplicity, directness, and intensity of his phrasing, as in the poem "The Summons of the Soul," an impassioned appeal to the soul of his lady to return.

O name broken piecemeal,
Strewn in the empty void.
Nameless name, deaf and dumb,
That suffers me to die as I call it.

The last word carved in my heart
Was never spoken in the end.
O you that I love,
O you that I love.

Crimson sun hangs on the west peak,
The deer bell and call sadly.
There on the sheer steep peak
I call your empty name.

I will still call your name
Until sorrow chokes and unmans me.
My voice goes aslant, rejected,
Lost between heaven and earth.

Were I to become a stone,
I would still call your name as I died.
O you that I love,
O you that I love.

The "name broken piecemeal," "Nameless name," and the vocative "you that I love" repeated four times easily lend themselves to more than a single reading. Whether he assumed the anonymity of a folk song writer or the individuality of a lyric persona in more personal pieces, Kim Sowŏl never lost sight of the function of the poet in an enslaved society: the preservation and extension of the hidden possibilities of language.

Poetry of resistance, voicing a defiant sorrow over the ruined land but speaking without violence or hatred, maintains a place. Yi Sanghwa (1900–1943), Yi Yuksa (1905–1944), and Yun Tong-ju (1917–1945) showed how to express in poetry their encounter with history and therein established the authority of the poet's expanded consciousness. Yi Yuksa's "The Wide Plain" opens with a story of the foundation, and goes on to deal with the beginnings of Korean history, stressing the inviolability of the land and its continuity.

On a distant day
When heaven first opened,
Somewhere a cock must have crowed.

No mountain ranges
Rushing to the longed-for sea
Could have dared to invade this land.

While busy seasons gust and fade
With endless time,
A great river first opens the way.

Now snow falls,
The fragrance of plum blossoms is far off.
I'll sow the seeds of my sad song here.

When a superman comes
On a white horse down the myriad years,
Let him sing aloud my song on the wide plain.

"Here" is modern Korea where the speaker utters his poem. "Now" is the winter of discontent and trial, the dark period of Japanese rule. The plum blossoms are a symbol of integrity, for they, as in China, are the first to blossom before the winter is over. The speaker sows the seeds of song in winter, in the belief that spring is not far behind, the day of liberation. Can anyone, like the superman, "sing aloud"? Who is "the superman," and what is his relationship to the speaker? It is perhaps the same as that between the lyric persona and "the traveler" in another of his poems, "Deep-Purple Grapes." The speaker is a prophet of the future myriad of years, a hundred years, or a moment.

Whereas Han Yong-un was Buddhist and Yi Yuksa was Confucian, Yun Tong-ju, who perished in Fukuoka prison, was Christian. Yun was an unimpassioned witness of national humiliation and degradation, especially the banishment of Koreans from the public realm of action, leaving only labor and work, to use Hannah Arendt's terms. Yun's poetry is pervaded by sadness in the face of a tyranny committed to destroying freedom and obliterating the integrity of the self. Embarking on a trying interior journey, with emptiness at the center of the self, he realizes that he must go out to confront his reality and let his wounds have voice. He tries to drive out darkness and awaits a morning "that will come like an era." Yun's brief but troubled life became a symbolic embodiment of national crisis, for he has shown what he has seen. Tormented by exile and a sense of unfulfillment, these poets knew they had to stand alone for a brief but significant life as against a long and obscure one. To be alive and a hero was unthinkable. But their pessimism was finally balanced with affirmation, and they celebrate in their work a triumph of self purchased with great sacrifice and suffering.

The first truly successful poet of modern Korea is Chŏng Chi-yong (b. 1903), a master of his medium and a continuing presence. Following Keats' stylistic advice, to "load every rift with ore," Chŏng renders particulars exactly: hard, clear, and Imagistic ("an intellectual and emotional complex in an instant of time"). Some of the effects of his best poems derive from the skillful use of onomatopoetic and other native expressions, which, when translated, unfortunately lose their original charm and force. The first collection of his poems (1935) was followed by *White Deer Lake* (1941), the high point of Chŏng's poetic career.

> *The sky rolls in the blue of White Deer Lake. Not even a crayfish stirs. A cow skirted around my feet disabled with fatigue. A wisp of chased cloud dims the lake. The lake on whose mirror I float daylong is lonesome. Waking and sleeping, I forget even my prayers.*
>
> *(sect. 9)*

The lake, like Thoreau's pond in *Walden,* becomes a figure of stillness and purity. Unlike a romantic naturalist like Thoreau, however, who is always haunted by moral ambiguities in nature, the speaker here describes "a condition of the spirit where the self is completely dissolved in the lucid apprehension of nature." Self and nature reflect each other, waking and sleeping become one. The collection represents the symbolic progress of the spirit to a condition of lucidity, the fusion of man and nature, as in classic Chinese mountain poetry. The arduous ascent to the summit of Mount Halla, where the White Deer Lake reposes, stands for the stages of spiritual pilgrimage, in archetypal themes of journey, quest, and initiation.

The force with which these poets observed the world and listened to the flow of Time in their blood—tradition—was a reflex of its hold on them. Unlike lesser poets who merely resurrected European movements and techniques, these poets delved into their own tradition to redeem the past and to verify a new world they created. The mode of reception of Symbolism is an example. They learned not so much its technique—which was nothing new—as the creation of new forms, the poem as an intimate experience of the individual artist, and an emphasis on the role of the intellect in poetic creation. They never lost sight of examining the immediacy of "now" and of reanimating

the Old to gain knowledge of the New ("Make it New"; *Analects,*
II, 11).

Advocates of Symbolism such as Kim Ŏk and his pupil Kim So-
wŏl, for example, reverted to their native folk traditions for greater
resonance in their works. A monk-poet, Han Yong-un, turned to
Buddhism and sang of the identity of the phenomenal world and the
ultimate truth, out of the intuitive wisdom that all beings are partici-
pants in the ultimate Emptiness. Likewise, Chŏng Chi-yong, a stu-
dent of Blake and Whitman and a convert to Catholicism, turned in
his mature poetry to his own tradition to discover a harmony between
man and nature. He therefore placed himself in the great tradition of
East Asian nature poetry, written in the first person singular, that al-
lows for the discovery of the self. Chŏng's poems unfold in the soli-
tude of nature, where one can best contemplate the interfusion of
man and nature, self and world. Again, poets of resistance who won
poetic victories with loss of their own blood depicted the spiritual
landscape through nature imagery, a veiled expression of nostalgia
for the stolen country. In addition to their contributions to the crea-
tion of a new literary language, as heirs of the tradition all these ma-
jor poets perfected the art of being themselves, a Korean voice issuing
from Korean soil with Korean themes. Gods of Korea are always Ko-
rean.

Among poets who came of age in the 1940s, some went north,
and some gave up writing. Generally, however, the liberation in 1945
ushered in a flowering of poetry of all kinds. I have chosen ten of
these poets, different from one another, each with a distinctive voice
and career, for they give a varying sense of how to survive as poet in a
divided and confused country. Some like Pak Tu-jin, Shin Tong-yŏp,
and Hwang Tong-gyu are determined to bear witness to the age.
Some like Sŏ Chŏng-ju, Pak Mogwŏl, and Shin Kyŏng-nim have
sought the further assimilation of tradition in varying degrees,
through the incorporation of unpoetic words, local and cultural ob-
jects, dialect, and other native modes of expression. Others like Kim
Su-yŏng, Kim Ch'un-su, Hwang Tong-gyu, and Chŏng Hyŏn-jong
have drawn on a number of Western traditions to enrich their work.
Also notable is the compelling voice of Kim Su-yŏng, who, with an
excruciating honesty and formal control, wrestled with his enemy,
generality—the established fact. Some are less touched by the exis-
tent reality than others, some are more dedicated to self-disclosure;
but all have sought their own voice for the sake of authentic testi-
mony, to reflect moments of their culture in crisis.

The constraints of censorship, which have driven poets to cover their immediate, urgent concerns, account for some of the elliptical associations and elusive metaphors. The steady encroachment of the politics of the age and other forms of repression have wrought spiritual havoc, but we recognize in the poets' gestures a voice that speaks to us. Their work bears the marks of desire, doubt, suffering, and frustration. Dismayed at the betrayal of hope and outraged at man's capacity for evil, some dwellers in this modern wasteland have become underground men, urban word-guerrillas. With a passionate concern for the fate of Korea, they have celebrated poetry, the quintessentially human. Despite considerable stylistic and thematic differences, they have opened Korean poetry to new areas of experience and have assimilated more of actuality.

Pak Tu-jin (b. 1916), who emerged in the early '40s as the heir of Chŏng Chi-yong and a member of the "Green Deer Group," wrote allegorical pieces in his early career to veil his love of country and to convey his vision of prelapsarian life. In his later poetry, he probed such issues as the relationship between knowledge and action, poetry and responsibility, art and freedom, to unmask brutal reality and the uncertainty besetting his society. "Soul-Sellers," a censure of folly in the Establishment and its servants, derides fawning flatterers and craven calumniators who, oblivious of their responsibilities, mock the conscience of divided Korea. Certain ways of life degrade humanity, and Pak exposes the deceived who buy affluence at the expense of human dignity. Modern toadyists, Pak says, are outdoing their forebears; they even sell their blood, sweat, vocal cords, ancestors, and brothers. He denounces their lack of self-awareness, the loss of integrity of the self. As a witness to the absurd history of a hypocritical society upheld in the name of democracy and modernization, Pak is a voice of conscience in the wilderness.

> *A dagger pointed at me,*
> *A cup of poison to be drained,*
> *I must embrace you.*
> *I shall open my burning heart to you,*
> *Digest you till my stomach turns,*
> *And walk to the heaven at the earth's end.*
> *One sun one moon*
> *Inextinguishable*
> *The timeless flow of water unending*
> *Till my soles harden into paws,*

This naked body will endure your lashes
Till flowers bloom everywhere.

The poet's world in "April" is the place of his origins, where he examines his plight as it reflects that of every thinking Korean caught up in the reality of the time. His strong moral passion and nobility of mind are revealed in the interior landscape, and his total awareness communicates the measure of his faith and belief. Unlike as in Eliot and Tate, April is not the season of despair: there is a hope of regeneration, a spiritual rebirth for contemporary Korea. Flowers will blossom again in the poet, and in us, when we have achieved a victory beyond suffering and sacrifice. The poet's quest continues, a quest for the meaning of life. It may be a long and dark search, but the voice of conscience has a civilizing power in a barbaric world which would frustrate the cry of the self.

The Silence of Love

HAN YONG-UN ⑦ 1879-1944

Translated by Sammy E. Solberg

THE EMBROIDERY'S SECRET

I LOVE "LOVE"

YOUR HEART

Han Yong-un

Han Yong-un, poet, patriot, and Buddhist monk, was born on September 29, 1879, in Hongsŏng, South Ch'ungch'ŏng, the second son of Han Ŭng-jun. He studied classical Chinese at a village school and is said to have astounded his teacher by finishing the text of the *Hsi-hsiang chi* (The romance of the western chamber) at the age of nine. He was married at fourteen and at eighteen took part in the Tonghak (Eastern Learning) rebellion (1896). He then fled to a hermitage on Mount Sŏrak, where he studied Buddhism and became a monk in 1905. In 1908, he went to Japan to observe the modernization process of the Buddhist church. In his essay "On the Revival of Korean Buddhism" (1910), he rejected the traditional ills of Korean Buddhism, preached that Buddhist reform could not be brought about without the regeneration of man, and strove to revive the faith. He also fought against the Japanese infiltration of the Korean Buddhist church and in 1914 published a digest of Buddhist doctrine in the vernacular. At the time of the 1919 Independence Movement, he helped draft the "Declaration of Independence" and signed the document as one of the thirty-three patriots. In prison he wrote another essay expounding the importance of Korean independence in the preservation of peace in East Asia. Released in March 1922, he continued his patriotic activities through public speaking and writing till his death of palsy on June 29, 1944, in the eastern suburbs of Seoul.

In May 1926 he published his single volume of poetry, *The Silence of Love (Nim ŭi ch'immuk)*, comprising eighty-eight poems plus "The Foreword" and "To the Reader." The collection was completed on August 29, 1925, at the Paektam Monastery on Mount Sŏrak. *Nim* is a complex word in Korean: in love poetry it is the beloved, in allegorical poetry, the king, and in religious verse, the god. In Han's poetry, *nim* is both the object and subject of love, be it the nation, life, the Buddha, or enlightenment. His poems are built upon a dialectic of engagement and withdrawal, motion and stillness, action and non-action, life and death, *nirvaṇā* and *saṁsāra*, enlightenment and illusion. His *nim* is the boundless *nim*, and it is with the one who is truly non-existent but mysteriously existent, the state which is permanent yet transient, that the speaker seeks reunion. His poems seem to make more sense when we see the true subject of his poems as the way of mystic experience, and the poet as a witness to the truth. Sam Solberg writes: "There is a sureness of touch, a constant awareness of the base, experiential and metaphysical, from which he works, that gives both substance and freedom to his poetry. In a very real sense his works are a 'making new' of the tradition, a powerfully modern poetry which is neither imitative nor forced."

In addition to poetry, Han wrote novels and treatises on Buddhism, all of which are included in his *Collected Works* (6 volumes, 1973). In 1967 a monument to him was erected in Seoul's Pagoda Park and a leading literary quarterly, *Ch'angjak kwa pip'yŏng* (Creation and Criticism), established the Manhae literary prize (1973) in his memory.

P.L.

PREFACE

The loved one is not only the beloved; it is also everything yearned for. If all living beings are the beloved for Śākyamuni, philosophy is the beloved for Kant. If the spring rain is the beloved for the rose, then Italy is the beloved for Mazzini. The loved one is not only that which I love but also that which loves me.

If love be freedom, the beloved also is freedom. But aren't you all bound helplessly by the high-sounding name of freedom? You have a love, even you? If so, it is no love, it is your shadow.

As I write these poems I am yearning for the lambs wandering the darkening plain searching for their lost way home.

YOUR SILENCE

You have gone. Ah, my love, you have gone.

Shattering the green brilliance of the mountain, hard as it might be, cutting off all ties, gone along the narrow path that opens out to the maple grove.

The old vows, firm and splendid as flowers of golden metal, have turned to dust and flown off in the breath of a sigh.

The memory of a sharp first *kiss* reversed the compass needle of my fate, stepped backward and faded.

I was deafened by your perfumed sounds and blinded by your flower-like face.

Love too is man's lot; even though we have prepared with fear of parting at meeting, parting comes upon us unawares and the startled heart bursts with a fresh sorrow.

However, since I know that to make parting the font of needless tears is to shatter love, I have transferred the irresistible power of sadness and poured it over my brow to quench the old ill with fresh hope.

Just as we fear parting when we meet, we believe we will meet again when we part.

Ah, even though you are gone I have never said good-bye.

The sad melody of my song of love curls around your silence.

PARTING IS BEAUTY'S CREATION

Parting is beauty's creation.

Parting's beauty is not in the substanceless gold of morning nor in
    the woofless black silk of night nor in deathless life, nor is it in
    the unfading blue flower of heaven.

Love, if it were not for parting I would not be able to live again in
    a smile, having once died in tears. Oh, parting,

Beauty is parting's creation.

I CANNOT KNOW

The paulownia leaf that gently ripples down the windless air—
   whose footprint is it?
The glimpse of blue sky through rents in the ominous black
   clouds driven away by the west wind after the tedium of the
   long rains—whose face is it?
The mysterious perfume caressing the quiet sky over the old stupa
   on its way from the green moss on the unflowering tree in the
   distant dingle—whose breath is it?
The small freshet, its source no one knows where, that winding
   splashes against the stones—whose song is it?
The afterglow adorns the setting sun with hands like white jade
   caressing the endless heavens, heels like lotus flowers set upon
   the boundless seas—whose poem is it?
The ash left after burning becomes oil again; my breast that burns
   and never stops—whose night does this weak lamp watch?

I WANT TO FORGET

Others say they think of their loves,
But I want to forget you.
The more I try to forget, the more I think of you.
Hoping to forget, I was thinking of you.

When I try to forget, I was thinking of you.

When I try to forget, you come to mind.
When I think of you, you won't be forgotten.
Should I give up both thinking and forgetting?
Should I leave forgetting and thinking to themselves?
No, that won't work either—
What can I do when you inhabit thought after thought?

If I really put my mind to forgetting
There's no reason why I can't—
Yet that means only death or sleep,
And I can do neither so long as there is you.

Ah, rather than thoughts that won't be forgotten
It is the wanting to forget that hurts more.

ARTIST

I am a clumsy painter.

Lying on my bed, sleep not coming, finger tracing across my
chest, I limned your nose, your lips, even the dimples that
spring in your cheeks.

Then, trying to limn the slight smile that ever hovers round your
eyes I rub it out a hundred times over.

I am not a skilled singer.

After the neighbors had all come back home and the crying of the
insects was stilled, I was about to sing the song you taught me
when I became shy of the dozing cat, and I dared not;

And so, as the passing wind fluttered the paper of the door, I
joined quietly in.

I don't seem to have the gifts of a lyric poet.

'Joy,' 'sorrow,' 'love': I don't want to write about such things.

Your face, your voice, your carriage, I want to write about those
as they are;

I also will write about your house, your bed, even the pebbles in
your flower garden.

THE PATH IS STOPPED

Your face is not the moon,
Still it crosses mountains and waters to shine into my heart.

Why is my reach too short
To touch your breast hovering before my eyes?

If you would come, what's to stop you?
If I would go, there's nothing to keep me, but
There's no ladder by the cliff,
No boat on the water.

Who was it took the ladder, destroyed the boat?
I shall place a ladder of jewels, form a boat of pearl.
I go on longing for you, the one who cannot come because the
    path is stopped.

BECOME ONE IN ME

Love, if you want to take my heart, please take me, and then, in
    the doing, make me become one in you.
But, if you'd rather not, don't give me pain only, give me your
    whole heart.
And then, give me your heart and your self, and, in the doing,
    make yourself one in me.
If not, give me back my heart and give me pain.
I will then love the pain you give me with my heart.

FERRYBOAT AND TRAVELER

I am the ferryboat
You the traveler.

You tread on me with muddy feet,
I embrace you and cross over the water.
When I embrace you, deeps or shallows or fast shooting rapids,
    I can cross over.

When you don't come I wait from dark to dawn, in the chill
    wind, the wet of snow and rain;
Once over the water you go on without a glance back.

No matter, I know that sooner or later you will come.
While I wait for you, day after day I go on growing older.

I am the ferryboat
You the traveler.

MY SONGS

There's no set measure, no fixed pitch for my songs.
They are out of tune with the melodies of this world.
But I'm not in the least bit grieved that my songs don't match
    common melodies;
Because my songs should be different from vulgar songs,
Melody modulates by force the deficiencies of song.
Melody is the chopping up of unnatural song with man's delusion.
To put melody to a genuine song is to disgrace the nature of song.
To make-up my love's face is to flaw it instead; to put melody to
    my songs is to flaw them likewise.
My songs make the god of love cry.
My songs squeeze rare clear water from the youth of a maid.
My songs become the music of the heavens when they enter your
    ears and become tears when they enter your dreams.

I know that you hear my songs far away across mountains and
    fields.
When my songs' rhythms tremble about to rise and fail to sound
    I know they enter your compassionate reverie and vanish.
When I think of my songs reaching out to you my poor heart
    throbs with an overflow of glory and writes out the notes of
    silence.

LIFE

Anchor and rudder lost, the small boat of life adrift on an angry
    sea, with the thread of hope of the as yet undiscovered,
    dreamed-of golden land as compass, course, and fair wind,
    sails the frightening sea where on one side waves beat against
    the sky, on the other against the land.
My love, take this poor life I dedicate to you and hold it tight.
Even though this poor life shatters against your breast, in that
    sacred land of happiness the pieces of my fully dedicated life
    will become the rarest of jewels, each fragment fitted to the
    next, decorating your breast, a badge of love.
My love! My life is like a tiny bird in an endless desert without
    even a branch to nest on; take it to your breast until it shat-
    ters.
And then, one by one, kiss the shards of my life.

AND YOU . . .

And you, why do you always smile when you look at me? I'd like
    to see your frowning face, but
For that I'd have to frown at you—I wouldn't want to frown at
    you; I know you wouldn't like my frowning face.
But when the falling peach blossom brushed your lips I felt like
    crying, not realizing I was creasing my brow;
And so I concealed my face with a gold-embroidered handker-
    chief.

"?"

Misty, dozing off, I was startled awake by the brisk step of my
    love, my eyelids weighing heavy still I opened the door and
    looked out.
A shower driven by the east wind passed over the spur of the
    mountains; in the sound of raindrops on the leaves of the
    plantains in the yard, now lingering waves of sound sway, then
    swing.
At the moment emotion and reason collide: the devil in human
    form, the beast in angel form, flash into sight only to disap-
    pear.

As you sang, drawing out the long tremolo, the poor half-awake
    dream of the young monkey lulled to sleep by the flowing
    tune is broken at the sound of falling petals.
The jewel-flower of the lonely lamp watching the night of death
    silently falls, unable to sustain its own weight.
Pitiable souls, burning with a mad blaze, explore for a new world
    at the north pole of despair.

Flower in the desert; full moon in the dark of the moon; face of
    my love.
My pure lips, unpolished jade though not rosebuds about to
    bloom, failed to touch your lips bathing in a smile.
In the window weighted over by the unwavering moonlight the
    shadow of a cat smoothing its coat curves up and down.

Ah, is it Buddha? Devil? Is life dust, dream, gold?
Little bird: little bird sleeping on a frail twig that sways in the
    wind, little bird.

SAND ROSE BY THE SEA

You said you would come before the roses bloomed. It is already
    late spring.
Before spring came I hoped it would come sooner, but now that
    it's come I fear it is too soon.

The innocent children clamored to tell me the rose was in bloom
    on the hill, and I pretended not to hear, but
You know, a mean spring breeze blew a flying petal against my
    mirror;
Listlessly I picked up the petal and touched it to my lips asking,
    "When did you bloom?"
The petal said nothing: through my tears it became two, became
    three.

WHICH IS THE TRUTH

As the sheer silk curtain swayed by a tiny breeze wraps around
    a young maiden's dream, your love that leaves no trace curls
    around my youth.
So as young blood dances to the beat, to the tune of a heavenly
    music, soft and pure, a small soul, gasping, goes to sleep in
    the shade of a flower-of-heaven, its petals falling silently.

As a fine spring rain, encircled by the hanging willows, turns into
    blue mist, so the thread of your love comes to weave itself
    around my sleep.
The short dreams are anxious to follow the wind under my quilt,
    and the dream voice calls out to the one across the river as it
    rides the swing in my throat.
As a slanting moonbeam breaks up the dew-wet flowering grove
    into white specks, so the sorrow of your departure has turned
    into a sharp knife cutting my heart to bits.

The stream just outside the gate has stopped flowing and lingers
    to augment its waves as it takes in my tears.
The mad wind from the spring hills stands waiting for my sigh to
    increase its power to shake down the petals.

AT THE SHRINE OF NON'GAE

Night and day the South River flows on, yet it stays.
Rain or shine Ch'oksŏk Tower stands vacant on the bank, yet flees
with time like an arrow.
Non'gae, you make me laugh, you make me cry, and I love you
for it.
You are one of the fine flowers that have bloomed on Korea's
grave; your fragrance knows no decay.
Becoming a poet, I became your lover.
Where are you? I know you live in this world yet I do not see you.

I think of your times, fragrant and touching like a flower cut by a
golden sword.
Soft strains that you sang, half-choked in the fragrance of wine,
moved the rotten sword, buried in the prison, to tears.
A chilling wind whirled the dancing sleeves, blew through the
flowerbeds in the land of the dead and froze the setting sun.
And your fragile heart, though calm, was more terrifying than had
you trembled.
Your beautiful guileless eyes, though smiling, were sadder even
than had you wept;
And your lips that were red went pale, then white, faintly
trembling—were they the smile of the morning cloud? Crying
of the evening rain? Secret of the moon at dawn? Symbol of
dew-flowers?
As you plucked with a soft slender hand some flowers by the
Terrace of Falling Flowers others you left standing blushed
with shame.

As your round white heels left their marks on the sloping river-
bank the old moss, arrogant and proud, soon covered their in-
scription with green candle-shades.
Ah—I call yours a house like a tomb, empty of you;
For without a house of your own, at least in name, how can I find
the chance to call your name?

While I love flowers, I cannot bear to break the flowers at your
   house,
For, were I to pluck the flowers at your house, my heart would be
   broken first.
I love flowers, but I can plant none at your house,
For, were I to do so, thorns would be planted in my breast first.

Forgive me, Non'gae. I broke the solemn pledge, not you.
Forgive me, Non'gae. You, not me, still shed tears of chagrin
   lying alone on a cold bed.
If I were to carve ''love'' in gold upon my heart to raise as a
   monument before your shrine, what comfort would it be to
   you?
If I were to brand my tears with melody and ring the ritual bell at
   your shrine, how would it absolve me?
At the least I can fulfill your final wish and for all time withold
   from other women the love I cannot give to you. I shall not
   forget my pledge as I shall not forget your face.
Forgive me, Non'gae. If you forgive me, my sins will vanish even
   if I do not confess before God.
Non'gae, who will live for a thousand autumns,
Non'gae, who cannot live even a day,
Just think how joyful I must be loving you, and how sad:
My laughter so great it turns to tears, my sorrow so great it turns
   to joy.
O, Non'gae, forgive me, my love.

THE SŎN MASTER'S SERMON

I heard the Master preach.
"Don't be chained to love and suffer. Instead, cut off the ties of
    love and you will rejoice in your heart." So he said in a loud
    voice.

That Master is a fool.
He does not know: true it hurts to be tied with love, but it will
    hurt more to cut the ties of love, it will hurt more even than
    death.
In the tight binding of love's bonds lies their unbinding.
Thus great liberation is to submit to the bonds themselves.
My love, I was afraid the rope of your love might be weak so I
    doubled the strands of my love for you.

INVERSE PROPORTION

Is your voice "silence"?
When you are not singing a song I hear your song's melody most
clearly!
Your voice is silence.

Is your face "darkness"?
When I shut my eyes I see your face most clearly!

Is your shadow "light"?
Your shadow is cast on the dark window after the moon has gone
down!
Your shadow is light.

THE EMBROIDERY'S SECRET

I have finished making your clothes.
I made your skirted coat, your cloak and your pajamas,
All but the embroidery on a little wallet.

That wallet is finger-stained
Because I worked on it, then set it aside, worked on it and set it
aside.
Others may think I have little skill in needlework, but there is no
one, other than myself, who knows this secret.
Whenever my heart aches I try to work on my embroidery, my
mind follows down the golden thread into the eye of my
needle, and out of the wallet a song flows crystal clear and
becomes my heart;
There is no treasure yet in this world that deserves to be kept in
the wallet.
I haven't finished embroidering the little wallet, not because I
don't want to—I have left it unfinished because I'd like to
finish.

I LOVE "LOVE"

Your face is a quiet star in a spring day—
But, there are also other faces like a new moon coming up
    through a break in the clouds.
If I loved only "winsome" faces, why would I embroider a star
    rather than the moon on my pillow?

Your heart is uncut jade, yet there are others whose hearts are
    firm, brilliant, and hard as a gem.
If I were to love only the beautiful heart, why wouldn't I set gems
    in my ring instead of jade?

Your poem reads like the new golden buds on a willow branch
    coming up after a spring rain,
Yet others have poems like lillies blossoming in an oily black sea.
If I were to love only good verse, why would I sing the praise of
    the willow rather than the flower?

When no one else in the world loved me, you alone loved me: I
    love you, I love your "love".

YOUR HEART

I've seen how black are your eyebrows, how shapely your ears.
Yet, I have not seen your heart.
When you were wrapping an apple you had picked for me, that
large red apple you wrapped so carefully, I clearly saw your
heart going into the apple.

I've seen your rounded belly and your lithe waist.
Yet, I have not seen your heart.
When you were looking at my picture and a woman's picture,
holding them in your hand, I clearly saw your heart turning
green between the two pictures.

I have seen how white are your toenails, how round your heels.
Yet, I have not seen your heart.
When you were putting my ring, set with a big stone, in your
small reticule, as you were about to leave, I clearly saw your
heart hiding behind the ring covering its face.

KIM SOWŎL ⑦ 1902-1934

Translated by David R. McCann

Kim Sowŏl

Kim Sowŏl is the most widely known and popular of twentieth-century Korean poets. The melancholy tone of his poems, most of which were published before he was twenty-five, and his use of traditional, "folksong-style" thematic and metrical elements combine to express poignantly a view of life that is felt to be particularly Korean. Many of his readers today find in his works an expression of the national sense of loss that was felt during the Japanese occupation of Korea.

Born on September 7, 1902, in Kwaksan, North P'yŏngan Province, northwest of P'yongyang, Kim came to Seoul to attend Paejae High School, graduating in 1923. Through the aid of his teacher and mentor, Kim Ŏk, Kim Sowŏl's poems were introduced to the literary world in 1922. In 1923 he went to Japan to enter Tokyo Commercial College but failed to pass the entrance examination; after lingering for some months in Tokyo, he returned to Seoul in the latter part of that year. He remained in Seoul during 1924 and 1925, trying, with Kim Ŏk's help, to make a career for himself in literature. Despite the publication of his poetry collection *Azaleas,* in 1925, Kim Sowŏl decided to leave Seoul. He returned in 1926 to his native region, to the town of Namsi, as manager of the local office of the *Tong-A* daily. Although poems of his continued to appear in the newspaper and a few other places, he had by this time effectively abandoned poetry. On December 24, 1934, he committed suicide.

In a lengthy "Remembrance of Sowŏl," published January 14, 1935, in the *Chŏson Chungang Ilbo,* Kim Ŏk described the stubborn, opinionated, and troubled young man he had known, a writer of brilliant creative gifts who expended great efforts revising his poems to achieve precisely the effect of tone and rhythm that he wanted. While observing that Sowŏl "hated to have himself called a folksong poet, and demanded that as a poet he be called a poet," Kim Ŏk nevertheless goes on to say that Sowŏl's skill was "incomparable in the folksong style." Kim Ŏk mentions that Sowŏl never had any close friends in the literary world; while this may help to account for Sowŏl's failure to make a career for himself in that world, at the same time it suggests something of the necessary difficulties that attended what he did accomplish. During the early '20's, when the rest of the Korean literary world was experimenting with the foreign literary styles then pouring into Korea, Kim Sowŏl alone, according to Kim Ŏk, continued to explore the resources of "the purest Korean . . . [in order to give] expression to his own, living poetic sentiments." This sense of personal integrity in the full body of his poems, coupled with an undeniable lyric gift, will continue to draw readers to his work.

D.M.

LONG FROM NOW

Long from now, if you should seek me,
I would tell you I have forgotten.

If you should blame me in your heart,
I would say "Missing you so, I have forgotten."

And if you should still reprove me,
"I couldn't believe you, so I have forgotten."

Unable to forget you today, or yesterday,
but long from now "I have forgotten."

THE GOLDEN MEADOW

Meadow
The meadow
The golden meadow:
Deep, deep in the mountains a stream of fire,
the golden meadow by my love's tomb.
Spring has come, the light of spring has come,
even to the tips of the willow's thread-like branches.
Spring light has come, the spring day
has come deep, deep in the mountains
to the golden meadow.

IN CHEMULP'O

NIGHT

True desolation, falling asleep alone.
Deep in my heart I long for you,
even as it appeared
that at last I would forget.

Here in Inch'ŏn, once called Chemulp'o,
the sun has faded into darkness.
As the night slows to a drizzle,
chill winds blow in off the sea.

Yet I lie down;
in silence, I lie down.
Pressing the shore, the high spring tide
runs pale against a blur of tears.

DAWN

With fallen leaves hiding my feet
I stood by the pool's edge
before the trees' dim reflections,
the eastern sky still dark, still dark.
Like tears of love, clouds flowed down
over my lonely dreams. And yet—

And yet, my love, a cloud has climbed
the east, glowing red, faintly red.
Fixed at the mid-point of the sky,
the old half moon fades into gray.

AZALEAS

When you leave,
weary of me,
without a word I shall gently let you go.

From Mt. Yak
in Yŏngbyŏn,
I shall gather armfuls of azaleas
and scatter them on your way.

Step by step
on the flowers placed before you
tread lightly, softly as you go.

When you leave,
weary of me,
though I die, I'll not let one tear fall.

THE ROAD AWAY

I miss you.
Should I tell you,
I would only miss you more.

Yet should I
leave without a word,
still again?

On the western hills as the sun sinks lower,
and in the fields, ravens cry.

The river's waters, flowing, tumbling down say
Come down, come follow away,
and still they flow away.

MOUNTAIN FLOWERS

Flowers on the mountain bloom,
the flowers bloom.
Fall, spring, and summer through,
the flowers bloom.

On the mountain,
the mountain,
the flowers blooming
are so far, so far away.

A small bird sings
on the mountain.
Friend of the flowers,
it lives on the mountain.

Flowers on the mountain fall,
the flowers fall.
Spring, summer, and autumn through,
the flowers fall.

WEDDING PILLOW

Clenched teeth grind
at thoughts of death.
Moonlight dapples
the window edge.

In restless sleep
tears drench her pillowing arm.
The spring pheasant, sleepless,
comes crying in the night.

The floating moon pillow—
Where is it kept?
On the pillow where two once slept
was a vow made for life and death?

In spring the cuckoo
by the foot of the hill
will cry enough,
my love, my love.

The floating moon pillow—
Where is it kept?
Moonlight dapples
the window edge.

THE CUCKOO

Cuckoo
cuckoo
my little brothers
cuckoo.

Our sister who lived by the Chindu River
returns, and calls to that village
by the river.

Long ago, far away in our land,
a step-mother's hatred killed our sister
who lived by the river.

Call to our sister,
Oh, in sadness! Our sister
tormented by jealous hate
died and became the cuckoo.

Remembering even in death
the nine brothers she left behind,
while others are sleeping, deep in the night
moving from hill to hill she sadly cries.

THE ROAD

Again last night
at a country inn
grackles screeched at dawn.

Today
how many miles
again lead where?

Away to the mountains,
to the plains?
With no place that calls me
I go nowhere.

Don't talk of my home,
Chŏngju Kwaksan,
for the train and the boat go there.

Hear me, wild geese in the sky:
Is there a road of the air
that you travel so sure?

Hear me, wild geese in the sky:
I stand at the center of the crossroads.
Again and again the paths branch,
but no way is mine.

FORSAKEN

In the dream I cried out
awakened
and came out to a field.

In the field a gentle misting rain,
frogs croaking
in deepening shadows.

I hesitate, hands clasped behind me,
nervously scanning the ground.

From within the firefly-swarming forest
someone calls out "I'm going; stay well!"
and sings.

BICYCLE

Night after night after night
I spread out my bed and lie down,
filled with longing for you.

The quilt's stiff edge
gnaws at my neck as I lie
filled with longing for you.

I roll myself up, but then
throw off the quilt and stand,
transfixed by the thought of seeing you.

How I wish I could see you!
But see, you think of me too,
longing and longing and unable to go.

The day after tomorrow
is Sunday;
Sunday, a holiday.

When the holiday is here
I'll hop on my bicycle
and go riding, rolling all around.

The bird that cries in the pines
on the hill behind my house
is the bird by your back door.

The bird cries cuckoo
                    cuckoo cuckoo.
Here cuckoo, there cuckoo.

Away in daylight
and returning at night, that call
is your voice longing for me.

The day after tomorrow, on Sunday
I'll hop on my bicycle
and go riding, rolling all around.

SAMSU KAPSAN

for Kim Ansŏ

What has brought me to Samsu Kapsan?
Here, the wild peaks,
waters tumbling down, the steeps piled up!
Alas, what place is this Samsu Kapsan?

Longing for my home,
I cannot go back.
Samsu Kapsan is so far, so far!
That ancient road to exile is here!

What place is Samsu Kapsan?
I came here, but cannot go.
There is no way back. If only
I were a bird I could get free!

I cannot go, cannot go
back to the home where my love stays.
To come or to go—the idea mocks me!
Alas, Samsu Kapsan imprisons me!

I long for home, but Samsu Kapsan
imprisons me.
No way back. For this body
from Samsu Kapsan there is no escape.

YI YUKSA ⑦ 1904-1944

Translated by Peter H. Lee

Yi Yuksa

Yi Yuksa—given name Wŏl-lok, Wŏn-sam, or Hwal—was born in Andong, North Kyŏngsang, on May 18, 1904. He was the fourteenth-generation descendant of Yi Hwang (1501–1571), a great Neo-Confucian philosopher of the Yi dynasty, and received the traditional Confucian education. In 1925 he joined the Ŭiyŏltan (an anti-Japanese secret society organized in 1919) and in 1926 enrolled in the Peking Military Academy. Upon return to Korea in 1927, he was implicated in the bombing of a branch office of the Korea Bank in Taegu and served a three-year term. His cell number was 264, pronounced *iyuk-sa* in Korean, or 64 *(yuksa)*, which he then adopted as his pen name. In 1930 he again went to China, where he was graduated in sociology from Peking University and met Lu Hsün (1881–1936). Upon return in 1933 he began his literary career and published poems, essays, and translations from modern Chinese verse and prose, including Lu Hsün's story "The Old Home" (*Ku-hsiang,* 1921). He was most productive from 1936 to 1940. In 1943, upon return from another visit to China, he was arrested by Japanese police and sent to Peking prison, where he perished on January 16, 1944.

On the slope of the Naktong River near Andong, his friends erected a monument in his memory (1968). A collection of his poems comprising thirty-four pieces (including three poems in Chinese) was published posthumously in 1946 (reprints in 1956, 1964, 1971, and 1975).

P.L.

DUSK

I lift the curtain in my back room
And welcome dusk reverently.
Like white gulls on the sea,
How alone man is!

Dusk, stretch out your soft hand,
I'd like to press my burning lips till sated,
Let me send my lips
To all that comes into your bosom,

Glittering stars in the Twelve Houses,
Nuns in the deep woods with vesper bells,
Prisoners on the cement floor,
Whose helpless hearts tremble,

Caravans trekking through the Gobi desert,
Native bowmen in the African forest—
While they're still in your bosom, dusk,
Leave the earth's half to my burning lips.

In my remote back room in May,
You'll have me lift the blue curtain tomorrow.
Secretly vanishing like the sound of a stream,
Will you return once you are cooled?

LET'S PRAISE A SINGLE STAR

Let's praise a star, a single star,
Not the many stars in the Twelve Houses.

Only a single star at dawn and dusk,
Our friend, shining bright,
A large eastern star, dream for a beautiful future.
To have one star is to have one earth,
On this old land of mottled sorrow
Let's sing till our veins burst
Of today's joy, our new earth.

Young night workers of war industry returning home,
Feeling the warm glow of girls' eyes,
Tired caravans yearning for a blue oasis—
You who pick stones in the fire-field,
Seek out a fertile land, be lords of the rich earth,
Sing a single star that belongs to all.

One star, one earth, on the stamped earth
Let us sow the seeds with our own hands,
And at the harvest of golden fruit and corn
Sing, wine-crazed, all ceremony set aside.

Some glorious God rules the weary and resigned,
We scorn dawn-seeking emigrants and scatter
Impeccable songs over the new earth like pearls.

Praise a star, a single star,
Let us praise all the stars in the Twelve Houses.

TRAVELOGUE

Life is a broken bark,
Scattered here and there,
Sloppy like a humid fishing village;
Only life's dust lifted,
An old mast.

Let others boast of youthful days,
Nightly my dream—
A smuggler junk in the western sea,
Bleached by salt, swollen by the tide,
No sooner clears a reef
Than fights a typhoon,
No sight of a fabled coral island,
Nor a Southern Cross.

The pursued mind, tired body
Climb the horizon at a stroke—
A sewer clutching my legs like tropical weeds.

A spider pushed forward by the tide,
I come clinging to a weathered shell,
Looking back on my life spent in far ports.

RIVER CROSSING SONG

On a moonlit December night
The river before me rang out, frozen,
As my song crossed the river and was gone.

Where the sky's edge meets the steppe
My song flew off like a swallow
With neither a lover nor a home to forget.
When its young wings wear out,
It will plunge into the sandy plain.

The endless blue sky covers the steppe,
Stars drink tears to mourn the dead.

Night weaves memory lovelier than a rainbow.
One melody is here, where is the other?
That night, my song crossed the river.

THE SUMMIT

Beaten by the bitter season's whip,
I am driven at last to this north.

I stand upon the sword-blade frost,
Where numb sky and plateau merge.

I do not know where to bend my knees,
Nor where to lay my vexed steps.

I cannot but close my eyes and think—
Winter
        Winter is a steel rainbow.

DEEP-PURPLE GRAPES

In July in my native land
Purple grapes ripen in the sun.

Village wisdom clusters on the vines
As distant skies enter each berry.

The sea below the sky opens its heart,
A white sail moves toward shore.

The traveler I long for would come then,
Wrapping his wayworn body with a blue robe.

If only I could share these grapes with him
I wouldn't mind if the juice wet my hands.

Child, take out a white linen napkin,
Spread it on our table's silver platter.

THE LAKE

My mind would dash and run
But my eyes, wind-washed, still meditate.

At times I invite swans, and unloose them;
Embracing the shores I weep at night.

As I ponder the shadow of a dim star,
Purple mist settles like a thinking cap.

A TALL TREE

Stretching to the blue sky,
Burned by time but standing tall—
Don't put on blossoms in the spring.

Brandishing old spiders' webs,
Fluttering on the path of an endless dream,
Your mind has no regret.

If you find dark shadows gloomy,
Tumble down into the lake's bottom
Where no wind can shake you!

LULLABY

My hometown should be lit by a million lights,
The grave grows moss and no yellow butterfly.

A dark dream gulps sorrow and pride,
Flowers of fire on the pipe are fragrant.

Smoke, like a shoaling-sail, circles the port;
Salt bleaches eyes at every familiar window.

Life is nothing if not wind and snowstorm,
Footsteps of a shadow returning after bitter wine.

Where does the river flow in a stifled heart?
The moon follows the river, I enter the cold river's heart.

My hometown should be lit by a million lights,
No yellow butterfly over the mossed grave.

PLANTAIN

Today, my sick breath is
An idle moon floating on silver waves.

Lift your blue skirt, plantain,
And wet my scorched lips.

Two fragments of soul scattered pledgeless
On the last days of the Saracens . . .

Where young women clung to the sleeves,
Lovely salt still weaves a dream.

Every time you saw far stars and new flowers,
How often have you dreamed of a lost season?

After a millennium, measure the
Persistence of autumn rain at night,

And when the rainbow arches the dawn sky,
Let us part again, aimlessly striding the rainbow.

MY MUSE

My shabby muse
Has not a single decent day.
His reign is that of night.

His groundless impertinence—
Everything is his, he says,
Flying over Indra's realm.

He never tells me about his home.
His pride is that he grew up
In the biting wind of the northern shore,
Traveled on the back of a dolphin.

A beard is an obstacle to courtship—
Drunk, he walks around a back alley,
Covering his large white ears with a cape.

For a thousand aeons,
By the rocky spring blue as melted jade,
He sings with straight voice when we drink,
And at cockcrow when he ascends
The star steps with huge strides—
I bed myself among the lilies,
Candleless, sleeves dew-drenched.

THE WIDE PLAIN

On a distant day
When heaven first opened,
Somewhere a cock must have crowed.

No mountain ranges
Rushing to the longed-for sea
Could have dared to invade this land.

While busy seasons gust and fade
With endless time,
A great river first opens the way.

Now snow falls,
The fragrance of plum blossoms is far off.
I'll sow the seeds of my sad song here.

When a superman comes
On a white horse down the myriad years,
Let him sing aloud my song on the wide plain.

FLOWER

In the east where the sky ends
And not even a drop of rain falls,
A flower blossoms red—
O endless day that will shape my life!

In the northern tundra at cold dawn
A bud stirs in the snow,
Waiting for a blinding flock of swallows.
O solemn promise!

Where waters seethe in the middle of the sea,
The flower castle erupts, fanned by the wind—
Today I summon you here,
My mob of memories drunk as butterflies.

CHŎNG CHI-YONG ⑦ 1903-?

Translated by Peter H. Lee

Chŏng Chi-yong

Chŏng Chi-yong was born in Okch'ŏn, North Ch'ungch'ŏng, on May 15, 1903, was graduated from Dōshisha University in Kyoto with a thesis on Blake, and introduced Blake and Whitman to Korea. He taught English at Hŭimun High School (1929–1945) and later at Ewha Woman's University, where he was dean of the School of Letters. He also lectured on the *Book of Songs* at the College of Arts and Sciences, Seoul National University.

Beginning his poetic career in the early '20s, Chŏng was active as a member of the coterie magazine *Poetry* (*Simunhak,* 1930–1931). A consummate artist, he produced poems marked by grace, precision of sensuous detail, and a masterful craftsmanship. As poetry editor first of the *Catholic Youth* (1933–1936) and later of *Literature* (*Munjang,* 1939–1941), he was responsible for bringing out talented younger poets, such as Yi Sang and the "Southern Trio." His prose poems in *White Deer Lake* (*Paengnoktam,* 1941, 1946) also exerted a great influence on the development of modern Korean poetry, especially on poets like Yun Tong-ju and Pak Tu-jin.

Chŏng was the first truly successful and versatile poet of modern Korea. He also wrote religious poetry as a convert to Catholicism, from which he was later estranged. After the liberation of 1945, he leaned toward the left but was unproductive as a poet. His two volumes of prose were published in 1949. He is presumed to have been killed during the Korean War.

P.L.

POMEGRANATE

Coals in the brazier burn lovely as a rose,
Spring night smells of dry burning grass.

I crack a pomegranate that passed a winter
To savor its kernel stones one by one.

O clear recollection, rainbow of new sorrow,
Soft and quick as a goldfish.

This fruit mellowed at the last harvest month
When our small story sprouted.

Young girl, frail friend, stealthily
A pair of jade rabbits doze on your bosom.

Fingers òf a white fish in an ancient lake,
Silver threads tremble, lithe and lonely.

Holding a pomegranate grain against the light,
I dream of a blue sky, Silla's myriad years.

GRANDPA

When grandpa
Goes out to the field
With a bamboo pipe,
A nasty day
Turns clear.

When grandpa
Goes out to the field
With a sedge cape,
A dry day
Turns to rain.

NEWS OF MAY

Don't you miss the early summer
Lighted by paulownia blossoms?

A young traveler's dream is a homing blue bird;
Under the tree or at the desk when I prop my brow,
Only memory rakes your old stories.
But at your welcome news my heart swells,
Every word splashing the distant Yellow Sea.
(I am wildly steering a dinghy, a gliding gull . . .)

With my cheerful May necktie as a fair wind,
Should I seek the romance of a lonely island
Rising out of a blue sea only the sky touches?

My small Pestalozzi, handsome as an oriole,
Teacher of Japanese and Arabic numbers,
Anxious waves might gnaw your island day and night—
Like a boom of breakers, with the sound of a far organ!

FEVER

The grape vine follows
The creeping smoke under the eaves.
Drought sinks into the earth,
Warm air coils down my back.
Ah, the child's burning with fever,
Gasping for air like a butterfly.
Pressing my lips against his tender head
And where a needle left its mark,
I mumble, I mumble
Like a shameless polytheist.
Ah, the child makes a fuss.
Moonless night, no light, no medicine,
Stars flitting like bees
In a far sky.

THE T'AEGŬK FAN

My baby may be running after a rubber ball
To a meadow where sheep call each other.

He may be dashing off a perilous bluff,
Hunting for a tiger swallowtail.

He may have grown wings and be gliding through the sky
Where dragonflies hold a fair.

Commanding birds, flowers, dolls,
A lead soldier, a locomotive engine,
He's a long-legged prince
On a sandbar by the sea, among the moon and stars.

(By the flowing river,
Stricken by unforeseen sorrow for him,
I'd often broken the reeds.)

Look at his silk breath,
Look at his dashing supple figure,
Look at his gourd-flower smile.
(I'm reminded of rice, money, and a leaking roof!)

Fireflies flit dimly,
The earthworms hiss like an oil lamp.
Amid gathering sultry winds,
A sorrowless fan flaps.

SUMMIT

On a sheer bluff,
Embossed cinnabar.
Dewy waters flow,
A red-plumed bird,
Perched perilously,
Pecks a berry.
Grape vines move past,
A scented flower snake
Dreams a plateau dream:
The granite brow, tall as death,
Where birds of passage return countless years,
Where a young moon sinks
And a double rainbow throws open a bridge—
Looking up, high as Orion.
Now I stand on the highest peak
Where star-sized white blossoms dangle,
My dandelion legs planted evenly.
As the sun rises, the eastern sea
Like a far flag fronting the wind
Flaps around my cheeks.

WINDOW, I

Something cold and sad haunts the window.
I dim the pane with my feverless steam.

It flaps its frozen wings, as if tamed,
I wipe the glass, wipe again—

Only black night ebbs, then dashes against it,
Moist stars etched like glittering jewels.

Polishing the window at night
Is a lonely, spellbinding affair.

With your lovely veins broken in the lung,
You flew away like a mountain bird!

WINDOW, II

I look out
Into a dark night.
A giant pine tree in the courtyard climbs.
I turn back and return to bed.

I'm thirsty.
I go back to the window
And peck the glass with my mouth,
Like a goldfish stifled in a bowl.

No star, no water, windy night—
The window rattles like a steamship.
Translucent purple hailstone,
Pinch my body, pound, shatter me!

My fever mounts.
Like a stricken lover,
I rub my cheeks against the glass
And drink in cold kisses.

O burning tinkle!
A distant flower!
A lovely fire breaks out
In the capital.

MOON

Through a paper screen that claims my eyes
The moon rushes in like a tide.

Released from foolish sleep on the pillow,
I go out when no one calls.

The garden I see alone at night
Brims like a round full lake.

White stone crouched in a corner,
How sleek and lovely its brow!

Light green shades, the color of dark india ink,
Their breath tangled in tired sleep.

Why do the doves call so anxiously?
Paulownia flowers, unbearably sweet.

CHANNEL

Through a shell-pierced porthole
The horizon swells to my brow.

A piece of sky settles
And broods like a huge hen.

I occupy an easily gotten seat
Before a parade of luminescent fish.

Like a conchshell my ears above the cape
Blow a tumultuous horn on a desert island.

A halo laps the channel's solitude at 2 a.m.,
Let's shed sorrowless tears like a girl.

My youth is my country,
Clear sky over tomorrow's harbor!

A sea voyage, I avow, seethes like love, and
Somewhere a sun blossoms in the moonlit night.

STAR

A star I gaze at from bed
Is far and high,

So near flickering lids,
As if joined by a golden skein.

Awake, I look furtively,
Pressed against the window.

Suddenly, gushing forth,
As if called out, invited in,

A lonely fire in my soul blossoms
In a whirl of contrition.

I get up with white pajamas on,
Fold my hands on my chest.

PHOENIX

I can neither name nor elucidate you.
You have nested in my inmost heart.

Wingless bird, an embedded arrow,
I know your sad cries and pained gestures.

I cannot send you away—no one wants you.
Truly, happiness is your enemy.

Have you indeed possessed my heart?
My bride! I've sealed my window and my laughter.

One day you died when my youth was spent.
Where is the stone that marks your grave?

Spreading wings amid a mound of ashes,
O sorrow, your phoenix, my tears!

WHITE DEER LAKE

1

Nearer the summit, the fainter the scent of gaudy flowers. As I climb, their waists vanish, then their necks, and finally only their faces peek, etched in patterns. Where a chill air matches that of the north, plants vanish, but are resplendent like stars strewn in the August sky. Fall evening shadows, stars light up in the bed of flowers. Stars move, I am bone-tired.

2

I have revived after wetting my throat with the lovely fruit of mountain orchids.

3

A white birch turns into a skeleton beside another white birch. I won't mind turning white as a birch after death.

4

In a demon-deserted desolate corner, ghostly flowers turn blue in the face.

5

At 6,000 feet, horses and cows mingle with men. Horse with horse, cow with cow, a pony follows a cow, a calf a mare—but they part.

6

A cow had a hard time at first calving. In confusion she ran a hundred *ri* downhill to Sŏgwip'o. The motherless calf moos, following persistently after a horse or a climber. Thinking of having to entrust our children to a strange mother, I wept.

7

Orchids' fragrance, orioles' call, whistle of Cheju birds, sound of water skittering over the rocks, pines at the ruffle of a distant sea. Among the ash trees, camellias, and overcup oaks, I missed my trail and emerged on a winding path, around the white rock covered with creepers. I ran into a mottled horse, which does not back away.

8

Flowering ferns, bracken, bellflowers, wild asters, umbrella plants, bamboo, manna lichens, alpine plants with starlike bells—I digest them, am drunk on them, and fall into a doze. Yearning for the crystalline water of White Deer Lake, their procession on the range is more solemn than clouds. Beaten by showers, dried by rainbows, dyed by flowers, I put on fat.

9

The sky rolls in the blue of White Deer Lake. Not even a crayfish stirs. A cow skirted around my feet disabled with fatigue. A wisp of chased cloud dims the lake. The lake on whose mirror I float daylong is lonesome. Waking and sleeping, I forget even my prayers.

YUN TONG-JU ⑦ 1917-1945

Translated by Peter H. Lee

Yun Tong-ju

Yun Tong-ju was born on December 30, 1917, the eldest of four children, in Myŏngdong, North Kando. His childhood name was Haehwan. He began to publish children's poems from 1937 and is said to have planned the publication of his first collection in 1941. Upon graduation from Yŏnhŭi College in 1941, he entered Rikkyō University (1942), then transferred to Dōshisha University in Kyoto, where he studied English literature. In July 1943 he was arrested by Japanese police on suspicion of subversive activities for Korean independence and died on February 16, 1945, in Fukuoka prison.

A monument was erected on the campus of Yonsei University in his memory (1968). His younger brother, Yun Il-chu, and his friend, Chŏng Pyŏng-uk, published a posthumous collection of his poems titled *Sky, Wind, Stars, and Poetry* (1948, 1955).

Yun's recurrent concerns, the sorrow of the oppressed and the presence of death, reflect the plight of the individual besieged by existential despair and spiritual desolation. An unimpassioned witness of the immense void following the collapse of old values, he realizes that it is futile to seek an illusive peace or relief. To be a poet is "a sad mandate"; but Yun has accepted his terrible fate and finds new ways of identifying his inner anguish with national crisis. His poems reflect that moment of his culture in crisis, and his short life is an embodiment of difficult times for his people.

P.L.

PROLOGUE

Looking up to heaven,
Let me feel no shame
Till the day of my death.
I grieved over the wind
That rose from the leaves.
I must love all death-bound things
With a heart that sings to the stars.
I must follow the path given me.
The wind grazes the stars again tonight.

THE SAD TRIBE

A white kerchief around her black hair,
White rubber shoes on her rough feet.

White coat and skirt hide her sad gestures,
A white sash tied around the thin waist.

SELF-PORTRAIT

I go round the foot of the mountain seeking a lone well by the
field, to look into it without words.

In the well the moon is bright, clouds flow, sky spreads open, a
blue wind blows, and there is autumn.

Also a young man is in the well. Hating him I turn away. But as I
go on I come to pity him.

When I return and look into the well again, that young man is
still there. I start to hate him again and turn away. But as I go
on, I come to long for him.

In the well the moon is bright, clouds flow, sky spreads open, the
blue wind blows, autumn reigns, a young man stands there.

AWFUL HOUR

Who is calling me?

I still breathe
In the shade of a budding tree.

I've never raised my hand,
I've no heaven to mark.

I have no place under any heaven.
Why are you calling me?

The morning I die, after my task's done,
Heartless leaves will fall—
Don't call me.

THE CROSS

Pursuing sunlight
Is hung on the cross
Atop a church.

How can you climb
A steeple this high?

No bell tolls—
I'll pace back and forth and whistle.

If a cross is permitted
To a tormented man
As to happy Christ,

Neck hanging down,
I'll spill silently
Blossoming blood
Under the darkening sky.

PRIMEVAL MORNING, I

It isn't a spring morning,
Nor one of summer, autumn, winter—
On such a morning,

A red flower blossoms
In the blue sunlight.

The night before,
The night before,
Everything has been settled.

Love with a serpent,
Poison with flowers.

PRIMEVAL MORNING, II

Snow lies white,
Telegraph poles howl,
I hear the voice of God.
What does it reveal?

When spring comes hastily,
I'll commit sin,
My eyes waking.

After Eve's toil of delivery,
Hiding my shame with fig leaves,
I will have sweat on my brow.

ANOTHER HOME

The night I returned home,
My bones followed me to my bed.

The dark room merged with the universe,
The wind blew like a voice from heaven.

Poring over my bones
That glow quietly in the dark,
I don't know whether it's myself that weeps,
My bones, or my beautiful soul.

A faithful dog
Barks all night at darkness.

The dog that barks at darkness
Must be chasing me.

Let's go, let's go,
Like someone pursued,
Let's go to another beautiful home
That my bones don't know about.

COUNTING THE STARS

Passage of seasons overhead—
The sky is full of autumn.

Without a single worry
I can almost count the stars.

I cannot count one by one
The stars etched in my heart,
Because dawn will break soon,
Because there's another night,
Because my youth is not yet spent.

Memory
    Love
        Solitude
            Yearning
                Poetry
                    Mother, mother—

Mother, I call each star by a lovely name—
Names of playmates who shared my desk,
Names of foreign girls, P'ei, Ching, and Yü,
Names of girls who have become mothers,
Names of my poor neighbors,
A dove, puppy, rabbit, donkey, deer—
And names of poets like Francis Jammes, Rainer Maria Rilke.

They are all far away
Like the dim stars above.

Mother,
You're far off in North Kando.

Yearning for the unknown,
I write my name
On the hill drenched with starlight
And cover it with earth.

Insects that chirp nightlong
Seem to lament my humble name.

When winter's over and spring comes to my star
—As the turf sprouts on the grave—
Grass will shoot up like pride
On the hill where I buried my name.

CONFESSIONS

My face reflected
In the rusted blue bronze mirror,
Full of disgrace—
Which dynasty's relic am I?

Let me shorten my confessions to a line
—Twenty years and one month,
With what hope have I lived?

Tomorrow, the day after, on that joyful day,
I must write another line of my confessions.
—In that youthful age,
Why such a shameful declaration?

Night after night let me polish
The mirror with my palms and soles.

Then a sad man's retreating figure,
Walking alone below a meteorite,
Will emerge from the mirror.

WHITE SHADOW

On a shadowed street corner
I give my strained ear
To the footsteps of twilight.

Was I so wise
To catch its steps?

Now that I've understood all,
I send off my many tormented selves
Buried deep in the heart
To their rightful places.

A white shadow vanishes
Around the corner into darkness,
White shadows,
The white shadows I once loved.

After sending away everything,
Empty-handed, I go round a back alley
To my room the color of twilight.

Like a faithful, placid sheep,
Let me nibble grass through the day, unperturbed.

FLOWING STREET

The fog flows, hanging low. Streets flow away. Where are the wheels of trams and cars going? A sinking street in the fog, freighted with sad passengers, no port in sight.

I stand holding a red mailbox on the curve, a faint light glimmers in the flowing city, the street light flickers, what does it mean? My beloved friends Pak and Kim, where are you now? The fog endlessly streams—

"We'll grasp hands again on a new morning!" After tossing a few lines down the box, I wait all night: a gold-badged, gold-buttoned postman will, like a giant, appear radiantly, a welcome visit, new as morning . . .

Tonight the fog keeps on flowing, blankly.

EASILY-WRITTEN POEM

A six-mat room in another country;
Night rain whispers outside the window.

To be a poet is a sad mandate.
Shall I scribble a line?

The envelope holding my college fees
Smells of sweat and love;

Clutching my notebooks,
I head for an old professor's lecture.

Come to think of it,
I've forgotten my childhood friends.

With what hope
Am I moving forward alone?

Life, they say, is hard,
I am ashamed
To have written a poem so easily.

A six-mat room in another country;
Night rain mutters outside the window.

With a lamp I drive out darkness,
The last "I" awaiting morning that will come like an era,

I stretch out my small hand to myself,
In a handshake of tears and comfort.

KIM KWANG-SŎP ⑦ 1905-1977

Translated by Edward D. Rockstein and Peter H. Lee

Kim Kwang-sŏp

Kim Kwang-sŏp was born on September 22, 1905 (1904 in the family register), in Kyŏngsŏng county, North Hamgyŏng, in northeast Korea. Upon graduation from Chungdong High School in Seoul (1924), he went to Tokyo, where he enrolled in the preparatory school of Waseda University and eventually was graduated from Waseda in English literature, with a thesis on John Galsworthy as social dramatist (1932). Upon returning to Seoul, he began teaching at Chungdong High School. In 1941 he was charged with preaching anti-Japanese sentiments and was imprisoned until 1944. Active as a champion of anti-Leftist literary movements after the liberation, he held a number of high offices: director of the Information Service of the United States Military Government in Korea (1947), secretary of the Office of Public Information under Syngman Rhee (1948–1951), and vice-president of the Korean P.E.N. (1957, 1959, 1961). He was also president of two newspapers, professor at Kyŏnghŭi University (1952–1970), publisher of a monthly literary journal, *Free Literature* (*Chayu munhak,* 1956–1964), and recipient of the Culture Prize of the City of Seoul (1957), the Ministry of Culture and Public Information Prize (1970), and the Korean Academy of Art Prize (1974). He died on May 23, 1977.

Such early poems as "Longing," "Solitude," and "Sorrow," which reflect the anxiety, emptiness, and solitude of a young intellectual under occupation and caught up by the Manchurian incident (1931), formed part of his first collection, *Longing* (1938). Anti-romantic in temperament, he attempted to invest his work with ideological content, often drawing on abstract words of Chinese origin, and sought for a unity of form and content. He continued to delve into the well of his life and art—"I'll search for the source of flowers and fragrance in this lonely earth," he says in one poem—and continually refined his style in a wide range of subjects, as in his fourth volume, *Sŏngbuktong Pigeons* (1969). Despite the cerebral hemorrhage he suffered in 1965, Kim kept producing a mature poetry that reflects the reality of his times. In addition to five volumes of verse, he also published his *Collected Works* (1974) and a translation of the poetry of Pasternak (1958).

P.L.

LONELINESS

I
Was born as one of the living and am lying here

The other side of this narrow tomb are waves of unlimited air
Beneath a certain quiet rock where the sea is deep

I
Am like the tired fish.

The pure emotions and beautiful dreams drop off to sleep.
Fragments of the longed-for world are scattered about.

Only layers of thought of long centuries are leading me on.

Insensible night,
Strange timepiece,
You, too, must sleep!

LONGING

All fine words
    become mute orphans
    become dreams, become grief.

Something calls me
    after the trail of the winds
    that night when even the stars fell

In darkness like an oppressive dream—
    one distinct image
    looms among the myriad.

INDIVIDUALITY

From a poor mountain vale

Born as a single pebble
Even though incapable of becoming a great boulder

Or
Flowing as a single stream
Even though incapable of reaching the wide sea
Hold the moment which soars in infinity!

SORROW

Because of the light's flashing
       in the heart of the sea
The night sea
       is utterly dark.

Waves
Slap and crash on the rocks
       beneath my feet
Freedom
Increases everlasting sorrow
       again in this land.

The gulls' cries
       distantly grazing the gloom
Come to my ears,
       gouge wounds in my breast,
       and disappear.

Ah, birds of poetry
       crying across the night sea,
Your way is cold
       and directionless in the dark,
Encompassing my agony,
       shall the poet of sorrow
Once again go off
       toward the night's great sea
       with you?

SUMMER MORNINGS AFTER RAIN

Days when the rain has cleared up
The crisp sky comes down into the pond
And fashions a summer morning;
Green shadows become paper
And the goldfish write poems.

CRICKET

In a spot tangled with yellow leaves,
With gray feelers
Groping the night and crying,
Comes a sir cricket

From within the woods of the soul
Imbibing heaven's dew,
A single phantom

The sky is high and the stars are distant,
The autumn winds are rustling and
Hidden within the season of falling leaves,
The crying of the cricket

The night, dark raiment
Humanity, wraiths
The cosmos are rumbling

LIFE IN THIRTEEN LINES

Globe turning while injuring me,
I was born in your wounds,
A squirrel scampering within a wheel,
Loves which fled into my rest period intrude

Within this mere box of a room
A mere soy bean of a light bulb
The emptiness of the East gathered below
Though this globe was washed with tears, there are remnants
Am I, too, an offspring of one of those drops?

On an empty chair in a diseased garden Death sits facing me
My thoughts smoke cigarettes
My feelings drink iced tea
Ah, let's set fire to the Twentieth Century!

LITTLE SONG OF THE SEA

Clouds fly, islands float, and the sky is blue
Within the coral halls of the deep jade sea
Beautiful secrets are hidden
On the golden sands the white clams are dreaming
Above the endlessly in-rushing waves
I go, boats go, and the wind goes, too

INK OF SYMBOLS

Transmuting
  Reality
    Into paper

While leading
  Love's
    Angel

My pen
  Draws black butterflies
    Spilling the ink symbolic

O = THE SYMBOL OF THE ELLIPSE

A shape come from where?
Your home is blue,
Are you the sign of finitude
Making boundless margins?

Endlessly deep ellipse
Within a white margin
A grateful eternity
Shooting off sparks

Following phantasms
A flood tide of wandering passions
Draped in heavenly robes
Hides in your heart.

Oh, seasonless mushroom that
Has set its jade throne
In the blue heavens,
Show your red tide of colors
Autumn
Touches your lips.

PUNISHMENT

I, Number 2,223
Draped in the garb of a prisoner
Wearing an alias on my chest
Sitting alone in the North Solitary Confinement Cell
Room 62 cellblock 3
Of the famous West Gate Penitentiary,
Ask myself,
"Am I Kwangsŏp?"

Three years and eight months
One thousand three hundred odd days
Without skipping a single day
Counting the hours on my fingers
With my manure bucket, washstand, and rag
With my chopsticks and enamelware bowl,
I've lived on the plank
In the dark of my fetid room

When summer is long and the days are muggy
I call for the sea and long for the mountains
My mind persistent as scallion kimch'i
Sets my tired, pent-up breath afire
And I want to burn, too

Pursued by the cold of long, long winter nights
When my back is cold and bent at the waist
More than sorrow or more than hunger
I felt the hairs on the back of my head, one by one
As though loaded with hoarfrost

Although now I'm living as Kwangsŏp,
Now I don't know what I've lost,
Now I don't know what I've gained and I just exist

However, though I stroll beneath the blue sky,
Suddenly incomprehensible darkness flies at me and
There is nothing more dismal for me than this

So when my eyelids somehow become rheumy
And I don't even know from where the tears are coming,
My tears, now, at last
Belong to fate even more than to love

As reparation for this darkness
With which human rights were trampled and freedom was pun-
    ished,
Japan, have you withdrawn?
As for me, though you give me your country, I'll spurn it.

LOOKING UP AT THE STARS

Away off there, twinkling,
    those stars
Where they come from,
    where they go
I have
    no desire to know

Scattered in
    endlessly vast space
Becoming friends and
    rejoicing in each other's glory,
Under sacred law
Effortlessly giving
    and receiving light

Eternally twinkling,
    those stars
All keeping station
    by themselves
All going their ways
    by themselves

Even if I have become a dim visitor
    to earth
To stand
    in some lonely spot,
If I could acquire a self-ruled
    soul,
I would be
    a star

SUNFLOWER

Fluttering with a silver sheen
    softer than the zephyr
The autumn sky's
    dizzying brilliance flows
And the sea is impressed
    upon the vast ether

Within a universe of emotion
    which cannot overflow this one heart
Radiantly blooming following
    the image of the white sun
Form sacrificing self
    in thoughts having run a hard-run day

Like Apollo's indomitable eye
    upon the well-spring of life
Adorned with layer after layer
    of golden powder of yellow petals
Ripening in a fragrance buried in
    the halo of the seeds of desire

In the joy of your lofty crown
    rising upon a single stalk
Receiver of Great Sol's blessings
    achieved every instant
Awe-inspiring petals filling me
    with wonder and with praise

SŎNGBUK PIGEONS

Sŏngbuk Hill has a new address,
As the pigeons, old residents, became homeless.
Trembling at the echoes from a quarry at dawn,
Your hearts crack.
You still wheel round in the blue morning sky,
God's thoroughfare,
As if you brought a message to villagers.

In the barren valley of Sŏngbuk Street,
Not a single wide garden
To light in and peck a bean,
Echoes from the quarry everywhere.
You take shelter on a roof,
Longing for the briquet smoke from the chimney.
When you return to the quarry, you rub
Your beaks against the rocks, still warm.

Pigeons, birds of love and peace,
Once men were sacred creatures
With whom to love and enjoy peace.
Now, you've lost the hill and men.
Where should we seek the love and peace you affirm?
Homeless drifting birds—

DISTANCE

I am a wall here,
You are a flower there.
Between you and me,
A slope of ice.

I dream of spring glow,
The slope melts away.
Wait—spring is far off.
Missing flowers,
I go to a florist—
Flowers follow me and sit on my table,
Spring too comes along.

Is there distance?
Spring will dissolve it.
Going or coming,
Distance is waiting.

MOUNTAINS

Strange—
The mountains near my home come down at dawn
Like cranes with outstretched wings.

The whole day crouching without food or sleep,
At dusk you fly off like wild geese
To distant places, leaving imprints behind.

Your flight does not bother
Birds' nests, flower petals,
Handfuls of earth,
Small stones in caverns.
You float calmly like the earth,
So birds, insects, and beasts are never alarmed.
Then the birds and beasts sleep soundly,
Dreaming of their own flight, as men do.

When men run knowing you will fly,
You are ahead of them.
It is kind of you to stop
For weary men to catch up.

You keep buried men on sunny slopes
And see gods worshiped on your summits.

Wishing to know men,
You enter villages with your feet.
But finding man's way of life muddled,
You go back home like a snail,
Raising your head and crawling.

You rule over man just as
You bring up trees and
Build sheer cliffs.

If lonely, you soar up to become peaks;
If you miss the sounds of water,
You descend and form deep gorges.

Only after a moment of rage
Can you become high, eminent pinnacles.

Spring always comes first at your slopes,
But a little way up there it is summer.
With you, the two seasons live in harmony.

SŎ CHŎNG-JU ⑦ 1915-

Translated by David R. McCann

Sŏ Chŏng-ju

Sŏ Chŏng-ju was born in the southwestern part of Korea, in the village of Sŏnun in North Chŏlla, in 1915. The southwest has had a distinctive flavor and reputation, exemplified historically by the late-nineteenth-century farmers rebellions and religious fervors, by guerilla activities continuing during this century, and culturally by dialect, cuisine, and a host of other subtle components of lifestyle. Sŏ's particular qualities as a writer have been seen as reflecting those of the place of his birth; the language of his poetry, its characteristic subjects, and the personality that emerges are as distinctive as the southwest itself.

In *Flower Snake* (1938), Sŏ has acknowledged the early influence of Baudelaire upon his work, which may be seen in the book's title, or in the "Poem of Sudaedong" where he speaks of an early love "troubling as Baudelaire." But through the exotic, "Western" tone and imagery of the early poems there emerges also an intense self-revelation that is, however, less factual statement than symbolic claim. For example, the first words of "Self-Portrait," "Father was a serf," can be read as curriculum vitae, or as a statement of Sŏ's independence from the literary world of the times, or as a statement of the condition of Korea under Japanese colonial rule.

Some of today's younger, urban poets of the "commitment" school have expressed the conviction that in the next stage of his work, Sŏ Chŏng-ju abandoned the issues of ordinary life and "retreated" into the past, or into more aesthetic concerns. In turning to the natural world, or to the past, especially the Buddhist past of the Silla era, Sŏ gave up certain of the themes and language that some readers of his early work have found most compelling. Yet for all the change in subject matter and theme, and the ostensible distance between the writer and his subjects—see, for example, "Snow Days," "Beside a Chrysanthemum," "Winter Sky," or "Rhododendron" —the scope of the poetry is broader, while the characteristic intensity of vision and expression remains undiminished.

In his most recent poems, Sŏ Chŏng-ju has returned to his own life. From a poem like "Snowy Night," one can look back on the course of his literary career and discover a remarkable parallel to Yeats: the early influence of late-nineteenth-century French poetry; the turning toward a legendary past; the spiritualism; the confrontation with age.

Sŏ Chŏng-ju combines intense passion, a highly refined aesthetic, and an earthy language and symbolism. He is the "most Korean" of contemporary poets because he has been most intensely himself.

D.M.

LEPER

Saddened by the sun
and blue of the sky

the leper ate a child
at moonrise by the barley fields

and through the night cried out
his sorrow red as a flower.

MIDDAY

A path through a field of red flowers
that plucked and tasted bring dreaming death;

along the path winding like the yellow back
of an opium-stunned snake
my love runs, calling me after

and I follow, receiving
in my two hands
the blood flowing sharp-scented from my nose.

In the broiling midday, hushed as night,
our two bodies burn.

SELF-PORTRAIT

Father was a serf;
he never came home, even late at night.
The only things standing there were grandmother, withered
and pale as leek root,
and one flowering date tree.
Mother, unmooned, longed for green apricots, even one.
By the oil lamp set in the dirt wall's niche
I was mother's boy, with black fingernails.
With my large eyes and thick hair
I am said to take after grandfather on my mother's side
who went off to sea, the story goes, sometime
during the year of reforms, and never returned.
For twenty-three years it is the wind that has raised the better part
    of me.
Life has become more and more an embarrassment.
Some read a convict in my eyes,
some an idiot in my mouth,
but I repent nothing.

Mornings, at dawn the drops of blood
mingle with the dew
of poetry fallen on my brow;
for I have come, tongue hanging out,
panting through sun and shade like a sick dog.

POSTCARD: TO A FRIEND

With my hair cut short
my face is not like a poet's.
I like the sky; I laugh
through my hard teeth,
and feel pleased as my fingernails
grow thick as tortoise shells.

Let us talk of the maiden
lovely as a cuckoo, my friend,
when you and I are dead
in the next world.
Why should we appear aristocratic,
like the slender-necked Li Po?

Even on Verlaine's moonlit night,
I braid rope with young Poktong.
If I should still hear the nightingale,
I will cut off my shameful ears.

BESIDE A CHRYSANTHEMUM

To bring one chrysanthemum
to flower, the cuckoo has cried
since spring.

To bring one chrysanthemum to bloom,
thunder has boomed
through black clouds.

Flower, like my sister returning
from distant, youthful byways
of throat-tight longing
to stand by this mirror:

for your yellow petals to open
last night such a frost fell,
and I could not sleep.

AUTUMN DAY'S REFRAIN

Persimmons along the hedge are dyed astringent;
cockscomb hollyhock, red.
How am I dyed this autumn day?

Last year's dipper gourds like big fists lie in the yard;
this year's tiny fists outside.
Where shall I lay my fist?

MY WIFE

That I not whirl about
my wife has set
out on the kitchen terrace
three thousand bowls of water.

My rumpled clothes
and *p'iri*—the sound of a breath
drawing the scent of cold water,
three thousand bowls.

If she should be first
to let her breath go,
I will obtain it
and pipe the *p'iri* full.

If I should be the first to climb
away into the skies, I will pour down
breath into her empty bowl.

ALLEYWAY

Day after day
come out and go
back through this alleyway.

Poor, broken-off
people watching the ground,
coming and going through this alley.

Not sad at all, the blue skies
cover this alley like a thin guilt.
Pale gourd flowers
blooming on roof tops.

Desolation
floods every nook.
When the wind blows
this alleyway shakes
as if in an instant
it would blow away.
Life in a hut,
or this alley, where P'alman
the beggar and Poktong live.
The older I grow the more
I cherish this alley.
I shall stay here a while,
then go on.

LOOKING AT A YI DYNASTY RICE BOWL

Seeing this plain porcelain bowl

    laundry hung on a line
    in the corner of my yard . . .

    white clothes, trousers and blouse
    I shall leave unfolded forever.

Like my brother
taken north during the war,
these clothes strung out
like a brother who will never
return
    I am ready now
    to have as they are.

OLD-FASHIONED HOURS

If this hour should be
your eyelashes
quietly blinking

fast in the shade
of the elm tree
I would be the core
of a single, ruby apple.

If this hour should be
the sharp clashing
of your fingernails

I would be an arrow
that lifted its wings and darted away.

But if this hour
is your snare, suspended
between the mountain and the river's gravel,

I am a lion who roars
and closes his eyes.

And if this hour
is your grandfather's chin-whiskers, stroked
once every forty-five minutes,
then I shall
drink *makkŏlli*.

RHODODENDRON

A mountain is reflected
in each petal of the rhododendron.

On the mountain's skirts
a sad concubine's house is napping.

On the porch is set out
a chamber pot of brass.

Beyond the mountain,
shoals of yellow fish in the high spring tide

and gulls that cry
at the pain of salt.

POEM OF SUDAEDONG

Changed into the old, white
cotton clothes . . .
Now my thoughts lean
by a chill, stone wall,
wrapped in the old ways
that seem remote as Koguryŏ.
Eyes closed. The dim
village of my soul returns,
and like stars emerging,
the strange, familiar ways of speech come back.

The lamp had been lit;
my life, long before
gone wrong. And that girl
from Seoul, disturbing as Baudelaire,
forgotten at last.

Number 14 Sudaedong, in the shadow
of Sŏnwang Hill: a house built of earth
by the clan head, the old man drying salt
in the Changsu River fields.

My mother excelled at clam-digging,
while father could carry huge loads on his back.
Just ten years ago
that girl was here, with me,
her hair held up with an ornamental pin,
wearing a green blouse for March.

Not long now. Spring
draws on, and I shall take that girl's
sister, her younger, dark-browed sister,
and live again in Sudaedong.

WINTER SKY

With a thousand nights' dream
I have rinsed clear the gentle brow
of my heart's love
to transplant it
into the heavens.
A fierce bird
knows, and in mimicry
arcs through the midwinter sky.

SNOW DAYS

Long, long ago my love fell asleep,
perhaps a thousand years before.

Wherever she is sleeping,
she sends me only the colors of her dreams.

Pink, soft pink
azalea hues of her spring dreams.

Red, deep red, the elm tree's red
in the murmuring hues of her summer dreams.

And now that snow is falling,
falling, and piling deep,
we are apart.

Woman resting by my side:
in the crescent moon that rises toward your finger's tip,
again my love's dream shines.

THE BRIDE

Just as the bride in her red skirt and grass-green blouse had loosened the hair by her ear and seated herself by the groom, in sudden haste he started up to relieve himself outside, and in his urgency caught the edge of his clothes on the door hinge. At this the groom became even more agitated, thinking the bride in her passion, unable to bear the delay, was holding him back. Aware of her, yet without turning to look back he hastened away, leaving a torn piece of clothing on the hinge.

Since then some forty or fifty years have passed. Happening to be near the house on some errand, he felt a brief pang of regret and opened the door to that room, to see the bride still with only the hair by her ear loosened, sitting with her green blouse and red skirt just like that first night. Touched with sadness he went and put his hand to her shoulder, at which she turned to ashes and crumbled away, crumbled away into grass green and red ashes.

THE HUGE WAVE

There was a day when the sea overflowed, climbing back up the stream, sliding through gaps in the hemp-stalk hedge, crossing over the corn patch to gather brimming in the yard of my grandmother's house. On such a day I would have been visiting for minnows or shrimp fry, and hopping around chirping, happy as a lark. Grandmother, who always seemed able to spin the stories out as long as the silkworm's thread, this time for some reason was utterly still. She stood there, her old face turned reddish, like the sunset, staring mutely out to sea. I did not understand, that day, but now that she has passed away I have at last begun to. Grandfather was a fisherman, sailing far out to sea, and one autumn, before the time I was born, they say that in a sudden storm he was swept away overboard and forever lost. There was simply nothing grandmother could say, though her face flushed red, when she saw the waters of her husband's sea returning to the yard of his own home.

SNOWY NIGHT

On Cheju Island where I spent
Christmas night my sixtieth year
wandering about
and met that girl in a wine house
by the shore—
she had learned my poem
"Beside a Chrysanthemum"
from her high school language book
and still could recite it perfectly.
When some pesky drinking friend said
"Here, come meet the writer,"
she drew to my side and hid
her eyes in the folds of my coat,
sobbing—that child:
Is she crying somewhere still as the snow falls this night?
Or have her tears dried? Has she learned to laugh out loud?

PAK TU-JIN ⑦ 1916-

Translated by Peter H. Lee and Sammy E. Solberg

Pak Tu-jin

Pak Tu-jin was born in Ansŏng, Kyŏnggi province, on March 10, 1916, and made his literary debut in 1939 as one of the "Southern Trio." From 1941 to 1945, because of Japanese repression and the prohibition of the use of the Korean language, he refused to publish. In 1949 he published his first collection, *The Sun (Hae)*. In addition to ten books of poetry, he has published essays and interpretations of his own poems. He is an accomplished calligrapher and also a connoisseur of stones, the subject of some two hundred poems. Currently he is professor of Korean literature at Yonsei University. His many awards include the Free Literature Prize (1956), Culture Prize of the City of Seoul (1962), March First Literature Prize (1970), and the Korean Academy of Art Prize (1976).

Upon reading Pak's early poems, Chŏng Chi-yong, the poetry editor of *Literature (Munjang),* commented, "Your poetry smells like plants in a forest . . . and brings a new nature to Korean poetry." Through a skillful use of such elemental imagery as mountain, river, ocean, star, sun, and sky, he summons hope for a new life, a prelapsarian world, a cosmos of perfect harmony. His later poems bear testimony to the existent reality and are imbued with a strong historical and cultural awareness. A genuine successor of the East Asian eremitic tradition, Pak has consistently rejected the false allegiances demanded by a squalid society.

P.L.

HYANGHYŎN

Beyond the mountain thick with dwarf pines lies a huge mountain, and beyond that yet another I can't see—my mind rides on the clouds.

The towering mountain, the massive, prostrate mountain, with every valley walled by long pines, the ledges overgrown with wild grapevine and onion; everywhere oak and rushes stand thick, and there badgers live, foxes, deer, rabbits, weasels, lizards, snakes—

Mountain, mountain, mountain, you have kept a long, tedious silence for countless years. Mountain, should I wait for the flame to leap out of your soaring peaks and prostrate ridges? Should I hope to see the day when foxes and wolves leap in joy with deer and rabbits to find bush clover and arrowroot?

HYMN TO THE GRAVEYARD

Even in the graveyard, sleek golden turf,
The rounded mounds are not lonely.

The white skulls shine in darkness,
The smell of death is fragrant.

Schooled in sorrow, the dead are not sad,
Longing only for the sun to shine in.

Granny-flowers in the golden grass, mountain birds.
The bodies rest in warm spring mounds.

MOUNT TOBONG

No mountain bird
Comes to call,

No cloud once gone
Returns.

Deserted place—
A shadow of a lone hill
In autumn dusk.

Hoy, hoy, I call,
No one in mind,

My echo rebounds
Across the empty valley.

The mountain shadow lengthens,
The red sun goes down,

Twilight will bring
Stars and night.

Life is the more lonely,
Love is only pain.

I embrace this long night and grieve
For your sake.

Where do you rest tonight,
In what village?

STARS

I've come this far through the mountains, fold upon fold. Without sign of life, bird or beast, through the bright midday valleys, I've come sunk in thought.

Among the bare branches of white birches, blown by winds like a white birch, washed by the sounds of water like stones, I've come hurrying, oblivious of solitude.

Dead trees stretch out their white limbs; crags, beaten by wind and snow, fly white clouds in the blue void.

Daylong gushing of water, swishing of winds, September leaves scattering petals on the blue lake.

I lodged in a fishing village on the eastern sea and under the blue-black night sky saw innumerable stars solemnly strewn across the sea.

Tonight from my hermitage I hope to see the stars again swept by cold winds, blossoming in splendor.

UNDER THE BLUE SKY

Come to me. Come to me quickly. There's a fire. Our sweet
homes are burning, green hills and gorgeous flowers are burn-
ing. Neighbors, our neighbors are chased and scattered crying.
No one left.

Wolves are howling. Sheep slaughtered. Wolves growl. Wolves
fight with wolves, tearing each other's flesh. Blood spills. They
kill each other, are killed by each other. Wolves fight among
wolves, wolves perish among wolves.

A gruesome night. But stars are in the sky, there are still stars.
Every day the sun rises. Come quickly. Dig up the waste land
and sow the seeds. Let us make the hills green, the flowerbed
pink.

Let's plant towering evergreens and annuals. Plant pines, plums,
peaches, wild roses, pinks, and wild chrysanthemums. They
will bud and bloom pink.

When golden birds light on the new green hills and butterflies
and bees swarm around pink flowerbeds, ah how happy you
will be with me. When the scattered neighbors return, ah how
happy you will be with me. Under the blue sky, under the
blue sky, let us dance and rejoice in the splendid flowerbed.
Let us dance and sing and rejoice. Let us cry and rejoice. Come
quickly.

PEACHES ARE IN BLOOM

Tell them that the peaches are in bloom and the apricots.
By the warm home you left abandoned, and now on that hedge
 once recklessly trampled, cherries and plums ripen.
Bees and butterflies praise the day, and the cuckoo sings by
 moonlight.
In the five continents and six oceans, O Ch'ŏl, beyond the hoofed
 clouds and winged skies, into which corner shall I look to
 stand face to face with you?
You are deaf to the sad note of my flute in the moonlit garden,
 and to my songs of dawn on the green peak.
Come, come quickly, on the day when the stars come and go your
 scattered brothers return one by one. Suni and your sisters, our
 friends, Maksoe and Poksuri, too, return.
Come, then, come with tears and blood, come with a blue flag,
 with pigeons and bouquets.
Come with the blue flag to the valley full of peach and apricot
 blossoms.
The south winds caress the barley fields where you and I once
 frolicked together, and among the milky clouds larks sing
 loud.
On the hill starred with shepherd's purse, lying on that green hill,
 Ch'ŏl, you will play on the grass flute, and I will dance a
 fabulous roc dance.
And rolling on the grass with Maksoe, Tori, and Poksuri, let us,
 let us unroll our happy days, rolling on the blue-green young
 grass.

SUN

Rising sun, sun uprising, clean laved face of the comely rising sun;
across the mountains, over the mountains you consumed the
dark, all night over the mountains ate up the dark, you comely
uprising sun with your ruddy unfledged face.

I do not like moonlit nights; moonlit nights displease me.
Frightful moonlight nights in tearlike valleys, hateful; fearful
moonlight nights in empty gardens, awful—

Sun, comely sun, when you come, only when you come am I hap-
py in the green hills, spreading their feathers, ruffling their
feathers, the green hills delight me; though I may be all alone
the green hills give me pleasure.

Following the deer, following the deer to the bright spot, the light
spot, following the deer; when I meet the deer I will sport
with the deer—

Following the banded tiger, following the banded tiger; when I
meet the tiger I will sport with the tiger—

Sun, comely sun, uprising sun, when I meet you it is no dream;
in one spot the flowers, the birds and beasts all sit down
together; I call them to sit together to relish the fresh and
goodly day.

PUTTING BABY TO SLEEP

Baby is crying
This baby will not go to sleep,
What is it? He cries on and on like a terror.
Kid with two bottom teeth
Breaking through like stars,
This kid with clear eyes bright as the morning star,
As if stung by a bee,
As if he had lost heaven and earth, all of a sudden—
Ah, what is it? He never stops crying like a terror.

Darkness fills the room like a rising tide.
The wind clings to the window and it rattles.
There's been no one by all day long,
In this corner of Seoul,
A corner like the deep mountains, baby cries.

I try singing a lullaby. Still he cries.
I try a marching tune. Still he cries.
I try cradling him in my arm. Still he cries.

    Sleep, sleep—sleep, sleep

In that distant childhood my mother sang me to sleep with an old
    lullaby,
A familiar folk tune,
Now I've tried singing it all through. Still he cries.
Then I try doing nothing. Still he cries.

    Chaboom, boom—chaboom
    Chaboom, boom—chaboom

I try bouncing him on my back. Still he cries.
Ah, there's nothing else I can do. Still he cries.
By now baby's mother

Rubbing her swollen breast—
   Ready to cry—what street is she taking?

Maybe baby cries from hunger he can't bear.
Maybe baby cries for his mother's breast.
Maybe baby cries for cold feet and hands.
Maybe this baby cries for fear of the dark room.
Or, maybe, this baby
Is sick of it all,
Of the world and everything in it, and that's why he cries.
Or it may be my state, my appearance, his shabby father,
Maybe he's sick of it all and that's why he cries.
Or, maybe this baby
Sees a hard life ahead
Growing harder as he goes on
And all the sadness of it, and that's why he cries.

I hitch the crying baby on my back and go out in the yard.
Splendor of the stars across the heavens . . .
—Little one, look at the stars, look at the stars.
Of all those stars in the sky
Which star is watching over you?
Your father may be poor, but
One, two, three—three stars,
Tonight I'll show you three stars that watch over your father.

The first star is my love, blue as the iris,
When tears stream down they become a clear blue stream,
The second star is my love too, white as a lily,
When mother's milk flows the white milk becomes a long river,
The third star is my love too, a burning blood-red rose,
The blood that flows from the spear thrust becomes a river of love;
Do you see, that first star is your mother's star,
Do you see, that second star is my mother's star,
Do you see, that third star is my Lord's star?
Ah, even now those three stars are looking down on your tears.

The wind grows colder, the night grows late.
Somewhere on her way your mother must be watching those stars.

    Sleep, little one.

Cradled in the hands of the stars in the far heavens, hands that
    descend,
May the stars in your heavens that watch over you shine brighter
    than mine.
May the sun that shines from your heavens shine redder than
    mine.
May the hands you clasp in the world be warmer than those I
    have.
May your belly always be fuller than mine.
May your clothes always be warmer than mine.
May the land you live in always be freer than mine,
May the days of your life be more peaceful than mine,
May your heavens be more glorious than mine.

    Sleep, little one.

CROSSING THE MOUNTAIN RANGES

The mottled mountain ranges are backbones of beasts,
I course up each ridge like blood spurting.

Ordering my disheveled hair with the wind,
Biting the morning sun with my blue teeth,

My roar is a scream, my roar spurts fire,
Setting fire to every dead sleeping valley.

Let an arrow come and pierce my heart,
Let a poisoned arrow pierce it,

There's a young sun growing in my heart,
My sun grows, tender and young.

Washing my ears with the howling waves
Of the madly rushing distant sea,

Let us weep once for the falling sun,
Let's weep once for the coming sun.

AUGUST RIVER

The August river claps its hands,
The August river writhes,
The August river agonizes,
The river hides its brilliance.

The river remembers yesterday's sighs, tears, spilling of blood, and
    deaths,
Remembers the forked tongues and bloodied teeth of snakes and
    wolves
That harbor the wrath, supplications, and betrayals of yesterday.

Remembers the remote idea of the Milky Way, the brilliant solar
    system
And its golden sublimation.

For the sake of victory, attainment, fulfillment for all
It commits yesterday to today, today to tomorrow.

The river, the river of August is long and bright.
Full of spirit, slapping its hands, flying its flags,
It moves on, on to the vast sea.

RIVER OF SOLITUDE

The sun bleeds light on the river—
Night of brilliant fires
Set adrift by solitude.

Endless barter between beast and beast
For tomorrow's end.
Before a blue blade on the chopping block
Lie peace and liberty
Helpless.

A cat's fiery eyes,
A witness to this night
For distant tomorrow,
The bloody record
Spewed out from the throat of a crow.

Winds become wine,
Sunlight tears,
The master of ceremonies
For this world and the next
Is now silent.

The last bouquet
For the tomb and the wedding
Is a trampled sleet of despair.

How restful this night,
And gentle the tamed, colonized intellect.

The fluttering flag, a signal lowered,
Even clouds and winds rebel in the field.

At the solitary riverside
Where a dove perished,
Calling its mate,

An old, blind, bronze horse
Winnies tremulously
To the far dusk.

SOUL-SELLERS

Eighty percent servile spirit and the rest is gall.
From the times of fathers, grandfathers,
Great-grandfathers, great-great-grandfathers,
North, south, east, west,
You kowtowed, bowed, beseeched on your knees,
Gold, silver, ginseng, pineseeds, tigerskins, virgins,
What's more, blood and sweat,
What's more, vocal cords,
Even your kin, ancestors, and brothers,
You sold them to Chinks, Japs, Ruskies, Big-noses,

Toadyism, but among your kind ferocious as wild beasts,
Biting and killing one another, ruined from exhaustion.
Damn it, damn it!
In a land of beautiful sky and earth,
You repeat rotten examples,
Throwing away your soul and gall,
"Korea in the world," "First-class backward nation."
You sold your souls to south, north, east, west,
Your housekeeping is dirty as a dog's,
Heaven fold upon fold, earth layer upon layer
Wail with tears of blood.

HIGH MOUNTAIN PLANT

You live on a sheer riven cliff.
The dagger in my heart is a blossoming orchid
Curving through the thick fog and rain, shivering in the wind.
A fierce bird's torn wings mirrored in the cold moonlight,
The gorgeous flags, like a tide, engulfing the hill,
The mute roar, now fallen as flowers,
You live on the cliff this side of the silent abyss.
Gusts will blow again in the morning sky,
Revolution will overrun the earth, north south east west,
The dagger will stab the chain, the net, that night,
The creation's last light scattering flowers.
Orchid, you live on a cliff where the fog shivers.

APRIL

A dagger pointed at me,
A cup of poison to be drained,
I must embrace you.
I shall open my burning heart to you,
Digest you till my stomach turns,
And walk to the heaven at the earth's end.
One sun one moon
Inextinguishable
The timeless flow of water unending
Till my soles harden into paws,
This naked body will endure your lashes
Till flowers bloom everywhere.

REITERATION FOR TOMORROW'S MEMORY

These are beasts wearing human masks,
Men wearing animal masks,
The beasts with human masks.

Ruthless, with jagged teeth,
Poison-smeared claws, fiery eyes,
Blood-licking tongues, powerful jaws.

They live at night, live in the day.
Born where we're born, the same blood
Runs in their veins as in ours.
When the beasts rave night and day,

The cries of the fleeing sheep being slaughtered,
Of tomorrow's white bones trampled,
Blood spilled by the lost and deprived . . .

Their tomorrow is the same as ours.
In our storm of tomorrow
They brandish blades, eye for eye, tooth for tooth:
From the morning beyond the blood a new sea booms.

SONG

If you come to mind I think of you:
Blow a trumpet, alone, in the sunset plain;
Drunk from fallen flowers, tumble into sleep.
Pace back and forth, play with the ocean,
Try hard to forget all that I know.
Burn the moonlight with crackling flames,
Steal ten suns, and carrying them in my heart,
One night for something to do—plan a rebellion.

A MESSAGE FROM THE CRANE

On a deserted islet in the ocean
Stay even if the sun sets, and the moon
Stay even if winds howl and rain

During the day chat with waves
At night repeat the names of stars
Memorize the names of countless stars

Eat grass berries
Wet your throat with dewdrops

Weave your dress with flowers
Inscribe your syllables on the sand

Wait there
On that lonely island

Don't say my words are foolish
The words I send to the winds

Flying over the six oceans
I'll bring you back
The joy
Of wings growing from my shoulders
Of my flesh and bones

Till that day that morning
Wait

HEAVENLY LAKE

Sun, moon and stars come down to talk old stories.
One deer stands, listens, drinks and goes
Trees stand guard and hush the breeze
Sorrow of the far, far sea
Until the restless waves slumber
Gathering together in the monotony of endless aeons, ages

Sun, moon and stars come down to talk old stories.

SELF-PORTRAIT

Stones, rolling, strike me,
Sands, wind-swept, sting me,
Waves, swelling, buffet me,

Long long aeons of time,
Sunlight beats me,
Moonlight strikes me,
Dark night knocks me,
Starlight beats me,

Ah, fluttering, falling blossoms,
Flower petals pummel me,
Winds blast me,
A drizzle, shower, sleet pound me,
A fine snow, flaked snow, blizzard,
Hail pound me,

And wrath thrashes me,
Doubt, anxiety,
Solitude batter me,
Despair smashes me,

No, it's love that smites me,
Endless remorse
Endless waiting
Craving flail me,

Conscience, justice, sincerity break me,
Truth, peace,
Freedom break me,
My own people break me,

Timeless beauty
Art break me,

Jesus of Nazareth,
Lord Christ and Father,
Thy Word breaks me.

PAK MOGWŎL ⑦ 1916-1978

Translated by Peter H. Lee

ONE-COLORED ETERNITY

AN ORDINARY DAY

SKETCH

UNTITLED

AT THE CENTER

Pak Mogwŏl

Pak Mogwŏl was born in Kyŏngju on January 6, 1916, and made his literary debut in 1939 as one of the "Southern Trio." He was editor of the monthly poetry journal *The Image* (*Simsang,* October 1973-), professor of Korean literature at Hanyang University in Seoul, and a member of the Korean Academy of Arts. He died on March 24, 1978. In addition to five volumes of poetry and a *Selected Works* (10 vols., 1973), he published essays, translations, and children's poems, for which he is well known. His poems brought him many awards—the Free Literature Prize (1955), the Republic of Korea Literary Arts Prize (1968), and Culture Prize of the City of Seoul (1969).

Pak's early poems, written in folk song rhythms, re-created the local color of the South with effortless elegance and control. But from the late '50s he abandoned the quiet of the hills to find material for his poetry in the urban experience of ordinary citizens. His later works, which tend to prefer open forms and looser measures, are marked by a plain, natural, often powerful language, incorporating dialect. The least public of the "Southern Trio," Pak was preoccupied with the plight of modern man, his entrapment and search for meaning in an inhuman world.

P.L.

GREEN DEER

On a distant hill
Blue Cloud monastery
with an old tile roof

When spring snow melts
on Mount Purple Mist

Along the hill's twelve bends
elms break into leaf

In the bright eyes
of a green deer

A cloud
rolls

MOUNTAINS ENFOLD ME AND SAY

Mountains enfold me and say,
"Sow seeds for a living,
Till the fields for a living.

"Build a hut under the hill,
Raise sons and daughters,
Plant pumpkins on each side of a dirt wall,
Live like a wild briar,
A clump of mugwort."

Mountains enfold me and say,
"Life is a dying moon,
Live like a waning moon,
Live like a waning moon."

WILD PEACH BLOSSOMS, I

The hill is
Nine River Hill
purple stony

A pair of
wild peach blossoms
burst

In the stream's
crystal clear
melted spring snow

A doe
washes her feet.

WILD PEACH BLOSSOMS, II

The stony hill
lapped by purple mist

Quiet
daylong

On such a day
wild peach blossoms

In a hillside village
the sounds of water

Clamorous, down the slope,
birds warble, mountain birds

A sun-drenched girl
crossing March.

LOWERING THE COFFIN

We lowered the coffin with ropes
That tugged through my heart.
Lord
Receive him.
The Bible by his head,
I said goodbye, sprinkling
A handful of soil.

I've met him since in a dream—
His long-chinned face
Turned around: "Brother!"
I answered "Yes" with my whole being.
Perhaps he didn't hear it.
Where only I can hear you
Is a world of rains and snows.

Where have you gone,
With good, shy, kind eyes?
"Brother!"
I hear you call me;
My voice doesn't reach you.
This is a world where I hear the thud
If a fruit falls.

ON A CERTAIN DAY

"Poet" is an adjective
That's always before my name.
Frayed hat on my head
I wander through rainy streets.
It's too small to cover my body,
Too absurd to shelter the little ones
Who always look up to me.
Man is not meant to wear
Dry clothes alone.
Only dry hair
Brings me to grateful tears.

METAMORPHOSES

I become a tree,
Its lower half
Shorn of flowers.
I know
Its lonely weight.

I become a drop of water
That falls from the eaves.
I know
The rhythm of life.

I become a plate.
I know
The fullness of its hollow space.

I become a wind
Racing the night plain.
I know
Thirst's kicking and screaming,
Solitude's shout.

I become a seed
Embedded in fruit.
I know
The budding of faith,
Tomorrow's promise and reassurance.

I become a stone
That rolls in the riverbed.
I know
God's providence, his work.

I become a pen
With which I write.
I know
The joy of devotion and service.

At this moment
I become the whole,
Time expands,
Language awakens,
Life's meaning gathers to a point,
Emotion's swelling balance—
I am alive in all things.

EARLY APRIL

Everyman gives one ear
To the other world—
Flickering sound
Of what is not,
Footfalls.
On earth it's clear April.

Everyman gives one ear
To the boom of the other world.
A gathering
Of waves advancing,
Sand-guzzling
Waves rushing out—

Everyman is listening
To two sounds:
The wind in an empty cavern,
The earth's bright April.

A METEORITE

To bed.
When I turn to the wall,
A caress of forgetfulness.

That's the way it is.
A pleasant meteorite,
A burnt remainder is bound to be light.

My poems lighter than sponge,
Can they be called poetry?

I've no complaint about
My common days and nights,
My broad narrow taste!
Let me sleep.

When I turn to the wall,
Clouds and mist delight me,
Round my head a wind blows.

That's the way it is.
An inventory of conflagration,
A burnt remainder is always clean,
A light meteoric stone!

My poetry of tomorrow,
Flavorless but free—
Evening of my life.

SCRIBBLE

I've known since I was a child
The feel of rotten planks
I once scratched with my fingers.
I know that thirsty dryness
Of sand that doesn't mold with water.
All that decays turns fragile,
My legs turn numb,
My poems turn to sand.
With inborn aridity
And a boy's abiding artlessness,
I cannot leave untouched
Rotten planks in a deserted corner
Or a clean stretch of sand.
Absently I begin to doodle—
Inscription of a god's name.
Today innocent fingers carve eternity on the planks
And try to knead sand into a man.
This simple scribble,
This thirst,
This god's name I carve on the rotten planks.

THE DOOR

A door is flung open.
To hear all day the door opening behind my back
Makes me uneasy.
Uneasy because my life, like a torn window, flutters.
A door is flung open,
Then closed with a bang.
Because my children are small
Their life is an exercise
In opening and closing the door:
Their riotous growth,
Their disorderly movement.
It's a joy to open a door that can be opened.
But you can't open all doors.
A door is flung open.
That they can open the door means parents love them.
A door closes with a bang.
They don't know the silence and solitude
That scorch my back behind the closed door.
A door is flung open.
Opening the door all day makes me uneasy:
But it's also a blessing,
Because I know the solitude and despair
That scorch my back behind the unopenable door.

TASTE OF SOY SAUCE

Adults work with gloomy faces,
Children grow with sulky faces
While soy sauce jars on the sunny terrace
Gleam and glitter all day long.
Squalid life with nothing cheerful;
Children dragging their rubber shoes
Spend dreary days—
It's bright all day on the sunny terrace.
Who says life gives delight?
Who'd hunger for happiness?
We live out a given life,
Getting along somehow or other,
But year after year soy sauce
Tastes sweeter than honey.
Who in the world cares!
While we live so, life seems to mellow;
While living so, children grow helpful.
All day long on the sunny spot
Soy sauce mellows sweeter than honey.

TWO POLES

I spent last winter
In a chair
By the oil stove,
Watching flowers of fire.
I did not light the lamp
Even at night.
The crackling of life's flame,
The veil of divine mystery
Withdrew.
Only my face that watches
The center of the fire
Is mottled by
Swaying pattern of flame,
Of light and darkness.
On my face,
At times like a god,
At times like a devil,
The truth of both poles
Is mine.
In their stillness the poles
Commune with each other,
And beyond the curtains
Snow scatters till the earth's end.

A WINTER FAN

I officiate
At my pupil's wedding in the morning,
In the afternoon
I rub down an ink stick.
Now
Shall I draw an orchid
Or mountains and rivers?
On a white paper
The spreading ink is lonely.
Between the pink flower that adorned your lapel
And the white flower pinned at the same place,
A moment.
On a winter fan
My poem
My song—
Truth is lonely,
The winter sun sets in the spreading ink.

MY MIDNIGHT

Even metals gather rust,
The back alley is paved with cool shadow.

The world freezes,
Good faith
Buries the seed of inner fire.

I go down a stairway,
Arms folded.

Already
Those who must hide have hidden,
Those who must fall have fallen.
O clear world after such reckoning!

When I open my mouth,
It's breath not my words that steams.

Within that truth,
Nightly,
In a wilderness at our back
Which hands can't reach,
My midnight pole star!

ANOTHER ENTRANCE

People walk through the tunnel
On the road leading underground
Not knowing if they have lost something,
If they have gained something.
They descend the steps,
Then climb the steps to another entrance.
They change direction
And walk away to the other side.
They don't know the chill fatal loneliness
Of the underworld.
Only one who has guessed the contours of life
Suddenly looks at the entrance darker than death
With a frightened face,
And checks his feet.

FRAME

A picture set in a frame.
The face in the frame
Grows no beard.
A framed picture—
Fire without heat,
Flowers untrembling,
Shamanism of white eyes
In the realm of four corners,
The framed picture.
Poetry dies
Existence is bleached
Even death is
Framed
Sunk in black ribbon.
Only the bones scattered across the field
Are alive.

PEEL A TANGERINE

At night, I peel a tangerine,
A tangerine that I peel alone on a winter night.
My poetry
Can't grow on the tangerine tree
But to moisten the lips
Of my sick child
I peel the tangerine alone at midnight.

Our language
Lacks an adjective
For the loneliness that soaks my heart,
There is no word
For the loneliness of one
Who peels a tangerine at night,
One man's thin fingers
Soaked in the tangerine's midnight scent.

ONE-COLORED ETERNITY

My shoelace comes loose
In the harvest month when ears ring clear.
Between meaningless lines
My shoelace comes loose.
Under the sky
Where the waterway of life
That can't be like hack work
Gushes out
To become clouds
To become stones,
No matter how you live, life can't be full.
In the one-color eternity of the harvest month
My shoelace gets loose.
Among stones
Some become monuments.
Among monuments
Some become stones.

AN ORDINARY DAY

My age, my inner thirst,
Tells me to cut a stone
To mark my grave.
A stonemason cuts others' monuments,
But I do my own.
Poet or farmer,
One who polishes the stone
For his own grave becomes wise.
After all, we sleep inside the stone,
A clear reckoning, forgetfulness.
Winds caress the stone
Dyed by a sunset glow.

SKETCH

People go to their jobs
Holding plastic umbrellas,
Worrying about life,
Greeting one another.
Beneath the umbrellas
All their faces are wet.
Can they see
Their own umbrellas?
The contour of the lonely soul is
Invisible.
It drizzles,
The drizzle that will fall steadily
While they live.
People walk toward the tunnel,
Each holding a plastic umbrella
He can't see,
On Sejong Street,
Above ground.

UNTITLED

Where I sit is my place,
A field of gravel, a plain of sand.

On that rock
A gull perches,
Trying its wings, letting out cries.

Yesterday
I gazed on the rushing tide
And longed for others.

Today
I want to pack and go,
Looking at the floating clouds.

For everything,
Where it sits is its place.

From a crack in a cliff
A grassblade sprouts,

On a steep slope
A tree strikes root.

Every place
Leaves no trace, once gone—
Grasses, flowers, and all.

There
Where waves wash the rock,
The gull cries in the sky;

Here
Where I shook off the sand and rose,
Winds smooth and erase my trace.

AT THE CENTER

From the earth's end
Where clouds wet their wings
To the tundra
At the earth's other end
Where the ocean freezes,
At that center
A stone,
Kicked by my foot.
From the tip of the lotus rising like foam
To the sea of sulfur and fire,
At the center
A stone
Is kicked by my foot.
On the path of wind
And whales,
On today's stem of a waterlily
That will merge with the vein of water,
At the center of
Sun and moon
A stone is kicked by my foot.
O love
O love
O love
An instant, a billion kalpas
Open to a single congestion:
A moment,
A single stone
Kicked by my foot
With a thud.

KIM SU-YŎNG ⑦ 1921-1968

Translated by Peter H. Lee

Kim Su-yŏng

Kim Su-yŏng was born in Seoul on November 27, 1921, and studied Chinese as a child. In 1941 he enrolled in Tokyo Commercial College, but later returned to Korea to escape the conscription of Korean students into the Japanese army and eventually joined his family in Kirin, Manchuria, where they had relocated. Back in Seoul after the liberation, he was graduated in English literature from Yonsei University (1947). During the Korean War he was whisked away by the Communists (August 30, 1950), captured by U.N. Forces, and finally released from a P.O.W. camp in 1953. He then worked for a newspaper, raised poultry at home, and lectured at several universities (1966–1968). On June 15, 1968, he was hit by a bus and died the following day in the Red Cross Hospital. In addition to three volumes of poetry, he left critical essays, an unfinished novel, and translations of Emerson's essays.

Kim was an indefatigable seeker of freedom. He understood modernism not as mere exposure tactics of sensational avantgardism, but as the attitude of the spirit as it makes sense of reality. Art is a pursuit of the impossible; hence it is disquieting. His poetry is a record of that struggle, and his gift for irony and commitment to the creative power of language often turn his frustrations and failures into terrifying revelations.

P.L.

HARD LIFE OF CONFUCIUS

When a flower blossoms atop the fruit,
You jump rope and play.

I sought the emanation of a phenomenon,
But found this hard as planning a campaign.

Noodles—macaroni in Italian—
Is it easier to eat because of my revolt?

Friends, I'll now look steadily at
The physiologies of matter and matter,
Their number and limit,
Their stupidity and lucidity

And then I'll die.

THE GAME IN THE MOON

A top spins.
Before my enormous eyes
That love to watch
The miraculous existence of children and grown-ups,
A child spins a top.
As the tidy child is beautiful,
So is the child who plays.
Sunk in thought and forgetful of the host,
I wish the child would spin it once again.
My life in the capital, harried and harassed,
My life more novel than a novel—
Let me dump such thoughts,
Mindful of my age that sits composedly,
Mindful of the weight my age accords me.
I watch the top spinning
Till it becomes black and stands still.
Every other house is better off, more at ease;
Theirs seems like another world.
A top spins.
    Spins.
Watch the string at the bottom,
Then a string between the fingers,
One throw on the *ondol* floor
Makes the top spin, gray and soundless,
Like a game played in the moon
I've not seen for ages,
A top spins
And makes me cry.
In front of the host fatter than I,
Who sits beneath the jet plane poster,
I'm not the one to cry
But I need some revising of my fate, my mission,
I should not be so absent-minded.

The top spins as if mocking me.
I can bring to mind
A propeller more easily than a top . . .
Like a sage of ages ago,
The top spins before me,
More good than evil.
When I think about it, the top is sad—
For the power that propels you and me to spin,
For some common cause, I must stifle my sobs.
Is that why the top spins?
A top spins.
     Spins.

HELICOPTER

It was the poets of a foolish land
Who first realized how easy it is
To kick the dark earth, where
Every man is in agony, and fly.
Seeing the helicopter lift lighter than a balloon,
Those who could be surprised know sorrow,
But the unsurprised can also know sorrow.
Forgetful of their own language,
They've long spoken others',
Barely spoken it, only stammering.
The season of sorrow gulping sorrow,
Younger than such a youthful season,
Is your timeless physiology.
After July 1950 you came to our cramped mountains
(Though you were made long before, yet
Came here after the jets and cargo planes).
Because Lindbergh didn't use you in his cross-Atlantic flight,
We perceive the irony of East Asia in your body.
We see your sorrowful flight drawing an arc of sorrow
In our little garden or from inside a jar.
We guess readily how you look from above
At our pure, blind love.
"Helicopter, you are a creature of sorrow."
—Freedom
—Sorrow
On a limitless time so boundless in view—
Without mountain, sea, mud, quagmire, regrets,
Your emaciated body, limpid frame, even cells, nerves, eyeballs,
You expose them all and let them drop;
Or as you fly nimble as a mist,
Your bold intent has dignity and good will
To open yourself before looking at others.
In an ultra-animal world

Your ancestors, together with ours,
Husbanded the beautiful archetype of freedom's spirit,
Yours before we discovered and defined it.
Holding fast to the silence of humility you weep
Over the last chips of freedom you bequeath.

A FOLDING SCREEN

A screen cuts me off from everything.
Turning your back on the world
Like a dull person drunk with death,
Indifferent to everything—
On your deathlike surface
Is a dragon, and the sunset.
Sorrow is what you must sever, you say,
To fashion a flying waterfall and a lonely island
On a height higher than fiction.
Planted in a most difficult place,
Standing before me,
You block out death with death.
While I look at the screen
The moon behind my back pours down its light
On the seal of an old painter.

WORDS

The root of a tree sank deeper toward the winter.
Now my body is no longer mine,
Nor are my heartbeat, my cough, my chill,
Nor this house, my wife, my sons, my mother.
Today I work and worry again as before.
I do a day's work—earn money and quarrel—
But my life is a life already consigned,
My order an order of death,
The whole world changed into the value of death.

All distance shortens clownishly,
All questions vanish clownishly,
The world won't give a damn
About so many words I want to tell.

Because of these wordless words
I can't deal with my wife,
My sons and my friends,
So I keep my mouth sealed before this extreme difficulty,
Indulging in this terrible insincerity.

These wordless words
Sky's color, water's color, chance's color, chance's words,
The death-piercing puny words,
The words for death, the words serving death,
The words that most abhor simple honesty,
These almighty words—
The words of the winter and of the spring,
Now my words are no longer mine.

HA, THERE IS NO SHADOW . . .

Our enemies are not dashing
nor as violent as Kirk Douglas or Richard Widmark.
They're not wild villains,
even are good to some extent.
Masquerading as democrats,
they call themselves
good People,
lawfully Elected;
white-collar workers,
they ride the tram or in a car,
enter a restaurant,
drink wine and gossip,
sympathize with a sincere face,
scramble and dash off,
write up their copy, keep books,
go to a movie;
they have charm.
In short, they're beside us.

Our battleline is invisible.
That's why our battle is so hard.
Ours is not Dunkirk, Normandy, Yŏnhŭi Hill,
it's not on the map.
It can be inside our house,
at our work site,
on our block—
but invisible.

Ours is a scorched-earth strategy.
Unlike the bloody battle of Gunhill,
it's not lively or spectacular.
But we're always fighting,
morning, day, night, at meal times,
as we walk the streets, talk,
run a business, build streets;
as we travel, cry and laugh,
eat our greens,
smell the fish in the market;
when our belly is full, when thirsty,
when we love, sleep, dream,
when we're awake, awake, awake . . .
when we teach, go home from work,
when we synchronize our watches with a siren,
when we polish our shoes,
our battle goes on.

Our battle fills heaven and earth.
A democratic battle must be fought democratically.
As there's no shadow in heaven,
there is no shadow in a democratic battle.
Ha, there is no shadow!
Ha, that's it!
That's right.
Ahm, no doubt about it, of course—
uhm, uhm, what?
Ah, that's it, that's it, that's it.

WITH A FLY

To a sickly man like myself
Today's fly is no longer yesterday's.

Unwilling to shake off its routine,
I am still plagued by civilization.

At the chilly autumn winds,
Tradition, like a bird,
Has found a place to settle
In the shadows of trees.

To think of sickness,
To cling to sickness—
Is it because I'm still healthy
Because I harbor great sorrow
Because I have great leisure

Because I know how to die
Like the soundless sound of a fly
Glinting in a vast sunny place?

BLUE SKY

Once a poet envied
The freedom of a lark,
Its rule of the blue sky.

One who has ever soared
For the sake of freedom
Knows
Why the lark sings
Why freedom reeks blood
Why a revolution is lonely

Why revolution
Has to be lonely.

LOVE

Because of you I've learned love,
A love changeless in darkness or in light.

But your face
The instant it emerges from darkness into light
Passes away and then comes back
Your face is so uncertain

Like lightning
    Lightning
Your cracked face.

DO YOU KNOW?

Do you know
Why Li Po had to drink wine before he wrote a poem?

Do you know
Why a poor writer pastes his closet wall with pictures of Casals,
Graham, Schweitzer, and Epstein?

Do you know
Why old Robert Graves writes love lyrics?

Do you know
Why our maid smiles at me when my wife's out?

Do you know
Why at such times I just pick up the laundry thrown down by the
wind and put it back up?

Do you know
Why I speak only Seoul speech to people from the North or South
who strike me as foreigners?

Do you know
Why after the May Revolution I switched from Paegyang to
Arirang cigarettes and stuck a colored handkerchief in my shirt
pocket?

Do you know
Why I don't turn the lapel of my hemp shirt on the hottest day?

Do you know
Why I don't turn the lapel of my hemp shirt even when I'm
alone?

Do you know
Why I take a proper pose even when I'm drunk or sleepy?

Do you know?

DESPAIR

As scenery does not reflect upon scenery,
Nor mildew upon mildew,
Summer upon summer,
Speed upon speed;
As clumsiness and shame do not reflect upon themselves,
A wind comes from some other place,
At an unanticipated moment, relief,
And despair does not reflect upon itself to the end.

FLANNEL COAT

After a nap,
My flannel coat has become heavier.
The tattered coat of a beggar
Met rain yesterday;
A symbol of my labor,
O intimacy of my pipe and crumpled cigarettes
In a pocket the size of a bull's eye.
The upper and inside pockets
Contain no money but
A scrap of paper that serves as a ledger.
With lack of money I've long been intimate,
The coat's weight is the weight of want.
What else is in the pocket?
A pencil stub,
Wastepaper of dead memory, old recollections
That all year I've never unrolled.
I had no use for the left inside pocket—
Does it keep my thirst for repose?
A thirst for repose, my intimate friend.

WALKING OUT OF THE OLD PALACE

Why am I bitter only at trivial things?
Not at that palace or its debauchery,
But at 50-*won* charcoaled short ribs
That are nothing but fat,
Or the madam fat as a pig
Who serves beef soup with rice.
Not once have I protested openly
For the jailed novelist,
For freedom of speech,
Or against the sending of troops to Vietnam,
But instead snap at a night watchman
Who comes time and again for 30 *won*!

My bigoted tradition has a history,
It cuts across my path like an emotion.
At the 14th Field Hospital in a prisoners' camp,
Once I helped nurses make
Sponges and gauze pads.
An intelligence officer chaffed me,
"If you're a man, be a sentry."

Now my revolt is like making sponges and pads.
I give in to a dog's bark or whine,
I give in to my young boys' grumblings.
Fallen gingko leaves are the thorny field I walk.
In every respect I am standing back,
Not on the summit, but slightly aside,
And I know standing back is cowardly.

That's why my protest is petty,
Not to a barber, landowner, ward officer,
Block headman, but to a night watchman
For 20 *won,* 10 *won,* or one *won*—
Isn't it ridiculous?

Sand, how small I am.
Wind, dust, grass, how small I am.
Truly how small I am.

SNOW

Snow is alive,
The fallen snow is alive;
Snow fallen to the ground is alive.

Let's cough,
Young poets, let's cough,
Cough at the snow.
Let's cough with ease
For the snow to see.

Snow is alive,
For the soul and body oblivious of death
Snow is alive through the dawn.

Let's cough
Young poets, let's cough,
Look at the snow,
Spit out the phlegm
Gathered nightlong in the heart.

PETAL, I

Whom should I bow to?
      Something common but not to man
      Not much, just a little
      As corn shucks shake
      In the windless threshing yard

The neck of wind does not know
      It rises by itself
      Over the hill it touches
      The joy of touching the glorious hill
      The little joy turned to flower
      But only wakes up after a pause

It looks like life at the dying hour
      A petal falling after crushing a rock
      Revolution
      A rock that fell first
      A small petal that fell last

Like a small petal that slid falling last

PETAL, II

Give us flowers
    for our anguish
Give us flowers
    for contingency
Give us flowers
    for now, not then

Give us yellow flowers
    streaked ones
Give us yellow flowers
    blighted ones
Give us yellow flowers
    contagious with excitement

Receive yellow flowers
    to blot out the enemy
Receive yellow flowers
    for the sake of others
Receive yellow flowers
    for a great chance

Forget what you seek before flowers
    lest flowers' letters slant
Forget what you seek before flowers
    so their voices can ring true
Forget what you seek before flowers
    so their letters can slant again

Believe my words
    yellow flowers
Believe unseen words
    yellow flowers
Believe trembling words
    yellow flowers
Believe all forgotten flowers trembling forever
    ugly yellow flowers

GRASS

Grass lies down
Blown by the east wind
That drives rain.
It weeps at last,
Weeps louder at darkness,
Then lies down again.

Lying down
More quickly than the wind,
It weeps and rises
More quickly than wind.

Come clouds, grass lies down,
Even to its ankle and sole.
Lying down more slowly than the wind,
It rises before the wind,
Weeps later than the wind,
Laughs before the wind.
Cloudy—the root lies down.

KIM CH'UN-SU ⓝ 1922-

Translated by U-ch'ang Kim

AUTUMN EVENING

THE LOOK OF THE EYES

FLOWER

THE SEASON OF RAIN

THE FIG TREE AND POETRY

ON SNOW

HOMECOMING

IN AUTUMN

MY GOD

IT SNOWS IN THE VILLAGE OF CHAGALL

A WINTER DREAM

THE WINTER CHRYSANTHEMUM

POEM

THE CACTUS IN EARLY SPRING

A DREAMING DREAM

Kim Ch'un-su

Kim Ch'un-su was born on November 25, 1922, in Ch'ungmu, South Kyŏngsang. After secondary education in Seoul and Tokyo, he went to Nihon University (1940), where he studied creative writing until he was arrested by the Japanese police for harboring subversive ideas (1942). After six months' imprisonment, he was sent back to Korea. He then spent several years in hiding, in Buddhist temples; after the liberation, he assumed a more normal life, writing poetry and teaching at a secondary school and then at a college. Currently he is professor of Korean literature at Kyŏngbuk National University. He is the author of seven volumes of poetry and four volumes of essays and reviews.

The imagist surface in some of Kim's poems is not so much an outcome of visual or sensory attentiveness as a unique ability to combine ideas with imagist surface or to submerge ideas in images. His ideas are not ready-made abstract ones, but those inherently present in the most concrete aspects of the world. In reviewing his poetic career, Kim noted that he was once preoccupied with the problem of ideas—how to convey "Platonic ideas" in poetry—but then realized that a poetic idea could be expressed only by a concrete image, and that the image "existed somewhere beyond words." This realization led him to mistrust ideas while being intensely interested in what lies beyond language, and subsequently to abhor even images if they acted as some kind of objective correlative, a controlled framing of the concrete in an idea. Lately, Kim speaks of a "poetry of nonsense" as his ultimate objective, which would be analogous, for example, to the action painting of Jackson Pollock.

Kim's search has been for ideas, for images beyond ideas, and then for nonsense beyond ideas or language. What stands out throughout his search is his determination to get down to the concrete, to that which lies at the bottom of our experience of self and the world. This yearning for the concrete is another side of his mistrust of the abstract, the world of meaning or that of public pronouncements—a consequence of the existential nihilism caused by the Japanese oppression and the agony of the Korean War. The sense of concrete existence, felt so despairingly by Kim to be ineffable and yet beyond the grasp of the world's terrible forces, is the only defense against the brutalities of the ideologically organized collective actions of men. One respects the personal integrity in Kim's adherence to the concrete in the face of sanctimonious public stance-making, even though it makes him a poet of relatively narrow range, and the narrow sense of self may in turn account for the sentimentality underlying many of his poems.

U.K.

AUTUMN EVENING

That the gods grow strong as they are led
by angels' golden hands
which do not burn in earthly fire,
that some gods tear bodies with the nails
of darkness until they lie bleeding
from mouths, noses, and eyes
and others create out of spilled blood
the ineffable perfume of meaning—
you saw this, Rainer Maria Rilke.
That angels let flowers bloom
with the caress of their golden hands
which do not freeze even in winter,
that while a youth may lie dying,
another heart flutters to life at his death—
this, too, you saw.
You also saw how in dark times
the faithless bird must fly out of the cage
into the sky raining ashes of death.

THE LOOK OF THE EYES

Have they just skirted my eyes,
a wisp of cloud that bloomed and withered
over the hill, the shadow of wind
that sang to me once upon a day?
Where are they breathing now
and growing unseen?

The look of the eyes of the soldier
going away, marching to the war,
his look of fear—
                        where is it now?
Flowers fall but the echo stays,
lingering in the garden.
The eyes of the soldier going to war—
Did they leave their look,
unforgettable and forever,
in the dark night of a stone,
in the hidden heart
                        of a stone?

FLOWER

Before I called her by name,
she was nothing
but a gesture.

When I called her by name,
she came to me,
a flower by me.

As I called her by name,
I would have someone call me by name
as befits

this color, this fragrance.
I would go to him,
his flower by his voice.

We all yearn to become
an unforgettable meaning,
you to me, I to you.

THE SEASON OF RAIN

Nukeia, girl with spring in your eyes,
you are dead and the poet is dead, too,
who sang your praise in Greece,
and now rain falls.
          In the Mediterranean
under a milk-white sky, grapes are pressed,
juice oozing out under treading feet.
Nukeia, mildew has spread over your eyes
and fleas and bedbugs hatch their eggs
in the damp corners of the room.

Whose eyes are weeping these tears, Nukeia?
There is no home we can turn to.
Sewers flow darkly through the city.
Nukeia, girl with spring in your eyes,
you are dead, and on souls waiting
without hope, now rain falls.
Our memory falls wet on your eyes
and seeps down to the bowels of children
asleep in the leaky shacks of the slum.
And a rank stream flows from the bowels
of three hundred and sixty children.
You die three hundred and sixty times
and now the rain falls on,
forty days and forty nights.

THE FIG TREE AND POETRY

The winter sky disappears
to uncertain depth,
to azure that is and is not.
A fig tree stands stripped
of foliage and fruit.
What poetry reaches and does not reach
the winter bareness of the tree?
The foliage and the fruit fall
to time that passes.
What poetry reaches and does not reach
the winter bareness of the tree?

ON SNOW

You cannot say that snow is white
or light as down.
Snow is heavier than it looks.
It could be dark as smears
on our souls left by the hands of men.
It could be dark, I say.
Of course it is white.
It can be sickly white, rubbed,
scuffed on our nerve ends.
When I was seven, my eyes met
the eyes of Poktong and Sunam, my friends.
Even in winter, lyric fruit grew.
Not any more. In the harbor lies
a warship at anchor, loaded
with myriad tons of gloom.
You cannot say that snow is white
until it is beaten into the mire
and trodden underfoot.
Nor is it light as down.

HOMECOMING

Winds coax the forsythia to bloom
by the river and in the eyes,
mirroring the blue of the sky,
of the mountain rabbit chewing
the berries of pure mountain-red.
Rabbit, rabbit, you saw boots stamping
on the faces of ancestral ghosts.
Winds coax the figs to ripen.
The fig is in the sixth month,
but the mind of youth is wilted.
The fire our mothers make is warm as ever
in the tradition-rich furnaces,
but the mind of youth is wilted,
though still warm and pure.
Is it sad and drooping in the village
because our mothers still gather
pine needles for fuel,
not burning coal or petroleum
as modern city women do?
No, it is not that, not modern fuel
that is in the mind of youth.
Where there are no walls standing
and no innocence untarnished,
why should the flowers blush
as the girls did in the festivals?
Why should grass be sprouting
under a sky forever the same?

IN AUTUMN

We saw the blood of youth
spilled in the quickening month of April.
Now autumn comes and my poetry
will shed its feminine vanity
for the affliction of Rilke
at the ancient castle of Duino.
It is not fruit nor its sweetness
that is ripening to a fullness
but the darkness of the bullets
spilling the blood of youth in April.
It is the silence of darkness
that shall ripen in this autumn.

MY GOD

God of my love, you are old sorrow,
the carcass hanging in the butcher's shop
or a bronze pot sunk in the heart of a woman
from Russia the poet Rilke once knew.
God of my love, can I drive nails
through your hands and kill you on the cross?
Even if I did, you would not die, my God.
You are childlike innocence
disrobing in broad daylight,
the bean-green wind among the leaves
of the tall elm in the month of March.

IT SNOWS IN THE VILLAGE OF CHAGALL

It is March and it snows in the village
of Chagall. The blue veins newly budding
in the temples of a man yearning for spring
flutter faintly, and snow soothes him
as it dances down from the sky
on innumerable wings
to the roofs and chimneys of the village.
It is March and it snows, ripening
to olive color the winter fruit
the size of mice droppings.
At night the women of the village make
the most beautiful fire of the year.

Kim Ch'un-su 225

A WINTER DREAM

The anthracite gas, for a spell of time,
warms the body and blood of the poor man
and his musty bean soup in the evening
while he reads the day's news
and his son listens to the radio
from the neighbor's house;
on a winding path it steals away
to the earth's Jurassic layer.
At night the citizens of Seoul will see
in their dreams a bird with coral claws
and three dinosaurian hands of pure gold
alight on the lowest roofs of the winter city—
the bird the savants of the West named
Archaeopteryx.

THE WINTER CHRYSANTHEMUM

Near the back gate to the compound
of the Eighth United States Army
with OFF LIMITS hung on the barbed wire,
children are sitting around,
warming their bodies at a brush fire.
Their peters peer shrunk and shaking
like dark red boxthorn fruit.

For a lavish wedding
a pot of chrysanthemum sells
for three hundred *won*.

POEM

A thousand apples fall
into the depths of the sky.
A vast ocean fills the aquarium
where the goldfish and green weeds move.
On the other hand, the camellia
is wet in the December rain,
and love is like a broken nail
thrown on the dusty road.

THE CACTUS IN EARLY SPRING

With a breast and the lymph nodes removed
my wife lies unconscious.
I wonder, in her drugged sense
does she think she is being trundled down
the hallway to the operating room?
Time hovering over death
walks a hippopotamus
over my thin-ribbed chest.
Looking up, I see the cold budding
of a cactus beyond her white pillows.

A DREAMING DREAM

Water dripped from the ceiling
into the basin
rises to the sky and becomes rain
moistening the roots of wisteria
and hanging it with flowers.
Then, the flower and the green pods
float up the sky.
Water dripped from the ceiling
into the basin underneath
rises to the sky and one day, some day,
rains on the oak leaves
and on the scar of migraine in your head.

SHIN TONG-YŎP ⑦ 1930-1969

Translated by U-ch'ang Kim

TO HYANG

KEEP YOUR EYES CLEAR

GO, IF YOU CAN

NO

A LAND OPENING NEW

A HEAD OF DAY LILY

MARCH

LIKE CIGARETTE SMOKE

SELECTIONS FROM *The Kŭm River*

SPRING COMES

DRUNKEN SLEEP

Shin Tong-yŏp

Shin Tong-yŏp was born on August 18, 1930, in Puyŏ, South Ch'ungch'ŏng, the ancient capital of Paekche and a city rich with memories of the Tonghak rebellion. The historical associations of his native place often were important contexts for Shin's poetic examination of Korea when he began publishing in 1959. Retrospectively, we can say he was destined to become a poet of history. When he came to Seoul to attend Tan'guk University, he chose Korean history as his major. When he began to write poetry, his theme was Korean history, especially from the liberation through the post–Korean War period, which he viewed as a serious falling-off from the innocence and harmony of the premodern era. To him modern Korea was a harried, exploited victim of imperialistic powers which had crushed the harmonious life of an agrarian and communitarian country. Shin used history to mount a critique of his own times. Yet, in spite of his larger concerns with history and the age, he never lost a lyric tenderness, which sometimes slides into sentimentalism. His historical critique may at times appear simplistic, yet he speaks for an important part of the mind of Korea, his people's nationalistic aspirations. He died of liver cancer on April 7, 1969.

Shin published a collection of verse in 1963, a verse drama, a libretto for an opera, and a long narrative poem, *The Kŭm River* (1967), on the subject of the Tonghak rebellion. His *Collected Works,* published posthumously in 1975, contains all his writings.

U.K.

TO HYANG

Let us go back, Hyang, to the time
when your face sparkled in the village well
mornings and evenings,

to the twilight among the swaying millet
and laughter of men warm and hearty,
and you with a hoe, face twilight-flushed,

to the legendary ritual of women
talking, and pounding the family wash,
with their feet in the jade-clean water.

Let us look into our eyes, Hyang;
keep our souls from deceitful rainbow colors.
Let us go back to our village
with its elm and communal labor.
Before we are poisoned by the sleek life
of parasites and tinsel luxuries,
let us go back to the village, our home,
where eyes are bright as morning,
youth and health.

Hyang, stepping high on air, one trips and slips.
Your face is not for false airs and shows.
Keep life simple as wild asters,
as when you weeded bean rows, barefooted.
Let us go back to our primitive land,
to the village dance of the legend-rich past
danced under the moon with swirling skirts,
to the fresh earliness of the rippling streams,
to the land of our heart.

KEEP YOUR EYES CLEAR

Night falls on the city;
flowers of fire light the fields
and the outlying villages.

Snow falls on the will of the 60s.
The river flows darkly
by the squatting shanties.

Walk barefoot on the earth
of ennui and suffocation,
greed and blood.

The doves fall silver
on the Eastern Sea. At dawn
ready your plough for the virgin hills.

Snow falls on civilized darkness,
on hunted animals,
on this stifled generation.

Plough the ice and sow the seeds
deep in the earth
for the new spring of clear eyes.

GO, IF YOU CAN

Yes, narrowness, that's it. That's the trouble. Rise high and you will see the earth. Caught in the milling, swarming crowd, you are trapped by such this and such that. High up, the sky is clear. It is not easy to raise yourself high above the entangling undergrowth, but try.

Look! How heads bump against heads! That's how they bleed to death. The summer floods carried lives away, broken limbs rising and sinking. Rise high. You will see history, the tall ancient trees strung with spider webs.

Your field is overgrown with weeds. You will know that yours has been a field of shadows, running to waste, unsunned beneath other trees.

Yes, rise high, just a little. You will knock against the field in the skies, spilling sunlight. You will see, beyond the ridge, the saplings of tall trees growing in the field now forgotten. Go, if you can, to the dewy field of dawn. Late as it is, it is never too late.

NO

No,
I have never hated.
With the bright sun shining
on the mountain slopes,
how could I have had
dark thoughts?

No,
I have never suffered.
With music flowing like winds
over the mountain ridges,
how could I have wept
rainbow-bright tears?

No,
I have never loved.
Breathing the winds
from the roof of the earth,
how could I have loved
city ladies in all their clothes?

A LAND OPENING NEW

A single day's sun is enough
to melt the ice in your fingers
before it reaches the canal.

Smoothing and healing
the broken-backed leaves of grass,
one forgets the cascading fall of history.

Your eyes fly over the ridge
to the fields in the neutral zone,
dewy-wet and ready for the plough.

Throbbing breasts put down roots,
as one walks among the tall trees,
gunsmoke-blown, and hears new music.

A HEAD OF DAY LILY

Tap, tap—
I tap

this flower head
from the woods

and I sense the clear morning
it has long drunk,

the scent of flesh
under the silk gown.

Tap, tap—
I tap

and I hear the tap
echoing down the ages

and sense the dancers of old,
the smell of bean soup,

the dew-fresh years,
the threshing of barley.

Tap, tap—
I tap

the clear head
from the Three Hans,

the head that knew the love
of Han mountain girls.

MARCH

Winds blowing, blowing to the sky,
fanning the rot and retch,
and blowing to me

as I stop by a music hall,
feeling through my empty pocket
and vacantly looking at a bootblack

with a blackened face, a box on his shoulder,
walking among the litter of empty bottles,
liquor bottles from America;

as I squat before closed office doors,
making a cheap meal of noodles
(for empty stomachs don't make lovers),

winds blowing, tickling the nose
as they announce the coming of spring,
spring coming to Korea,

shall I go to Cheju before April comes?
Shall I go to the seashore
and dine on globefish eggs?

Winds blowing, villages wasting,
the flower-flesh of history rotting,
highrise buildings rising,

my brothers passing under the windows
of Kwanghwamun, saying nothing,
with their heads hanging,

filling the stomach with noodles,
spending the day on a bench in the park,
hearing a rumble as on the Yalu bridge,

arrogance from abroad mounting,
crap from the assholes of foreigners
burying their "Korea"—

am I alone now, walking
in front of foreign embassies
with clipped wings?

No, I am not alone
in this procession of hunger,
at this time of the year,

when not an inch of land is left
to stand on with ease and peace,
when only evil designs proliferate.

Feeling through empty pockets,
standing at a bus stop in Seoul,
vacantly listening,

listening to the spring of Asanyŏ
weeping like a cicada in the leaves,
and walking with a hang-dog head . . .

O Tonghak! Tonghak! By the unseeing Kŭm
the broken-throated spirit
in this time still unripe!

Shall I go before April comes
to the Sobaek Mountains,
against the ripeness of time

shall I wait out in the country,
living in the fields,
sharpening the spears of flowers?

LIKE CIGARETTE SMOKE

Like cigarette smoke on a field path,
all my yearning blew away.

There were many I wanted to love
but I stood by merely looking from afar.

Like cigarette smoke on a field path,
all my yearning blew away.

There was a family I wanted to love
but my love ended merely as a thought.

I drew water from a well inside
until the bucket broke.

There were many I wanted to love
but the blue of the sky beckoned

too soon, far too soon,
to another path in the fields.

Traveler, as you walk in the days to come
on this field path,

feel this sweet breeze
and know that in it was a breath

of a man who walked there once
but fell ill and left in the middle of his way—

greet the breath
with softening eyes.

SELECTIONS FROM *THE KŬM RIVER*

Prologue, 2

We saw Heaven
in the fourth month, 1960.
Rain clouds breaking
in the sky of history,
we saw Heaven,
the face of eternity.

Your face that shone a moment
was the heart deep inside us.

From the springs of the sky
we scooped a handful of water
and washed our face,
in 1919.

In 1894 your face shone
on the rocks, on the aged trees,
your face Heaven-full.
The blue of Heaven shone a moment,
only to be taken from us.
But then flowers bloomed
by the river and on the mountains;
the land was full of flowers, and sun,
the autumn of harvest,
young love and work.
The Eastern Sea, its bright-colored sands,
backpaths to India,
the ruins of ceramic kilns,
I visited them all with lame steps
on my vacations, wearing a mountain cap.
But there was nothing,
nothing in the outer world,
no unflawed porcelain,

no warm-blooded flesh;
there was nothing in the world.
But your face,
your face
of eternity
shone once,
your face
in the eternity of our hearts.

2

Suun, born in 1814, in Kyŏngsang province,
left his native place at sixteen
when he lost his parents.
He walked three thousand *ri*
in his straw sandals—a way of spirit,
of cracked lips, torn footsoles and knees;
he walked twenty years and saw—
hunger in the land,
maltreatment,
disease,
serfs dragged like oxen
by the nobility,
misgovernment,
the twilight of the Yi dynasty,
its skeletal decay.

Two thousand years ago,
in Israel where fire-rain fell,
a prophet arose
and died, nails in the ripe fruit.
Why?

Three thousand years ago
in the foothills of the Himalayas,
in the shade of a shining Bo tree,
a flower of humanity
felt sorrow,
blooming too early.

In the fourth month, 1860,
under the new-leaved persimmon tree,
Suun saw,
with joy that rived the rocks,
Heaven,
the shining Heaven of eternity.

4

Suun was arrested by the king's order
and sent to a prison in Taegu
to die a martyr's death
on the river banks of Nodŭl in Taegu.
It was the tenth of the third month, 1864.
Haewŏl went to see him in prison
by bribing the prison guards.
He tried to persuade Suun to escape,
but Suun sat quietly and did not listen.
He gave Haewŏl a tobacco pipe
with long bamboo stem for their parting.
In the evening of the same day
Haewŏl, the second Master of Eastern Learning,
broke open the bamboo-pipe of Suun
and read with Yi P'il, a brother in faith,
under the dim light of a tavern
the sesame-seed small handwriting
of the Master written on a scroll:

> *The light of the lamp shines on water;*
> *therefore it does not mind the distance.*
> *The pillar is like an aged tree*
> *but strength remains unchanged.*
> *Your mind is my mind.*
> *Our death is eternal*
> *as a pillar in the mansion.*
> *I follow the will of Heaven.*
> *You must fly to a distant land.*

While peasants made manure on the dunghill
which gave off white vapors
in the bright sunlight of morning,
Haewŏl, Yi P'il and several others,
clad as soldiers, fled passing
the fields of Sangju and through the path
of ninety-nine bends of the Bird Ranges.
They hid in the T'aebaek Mountains.
Meanwhile the king offered for their capture
a prize of a thousand silvers.
Suun left behind him two books:
Grand Outline of Eastern Learning
and *Remains of Master Yongdam.*
He wrote:

> *Man is Heaven.*
> *Slaves, peasants, untouchables,*
> *All men are Heaven.*
> *We live with Heaven in us,*
> *Heaven lives in us.*
> *When Heaven is outside us,*
> *it is wind, it is water.*
> *We realize Heaven in us*
> *but we cannot give it to others.*
> *All living beings,*
> *serve your neighbors*
> *as you serve Heaven.*

Suun had two slaves in his family.
He freed them, marrying one to his son
and adopting the other as his daughter.
He had rich lands inherited from his father;
he gave them away to landless peasants.

7

We leave life as if on a journey.
What is finished is just as well
either one way or another.
Now at this moment the suffering
of the diseased and the hurt
who cannot sleep even at night
tosses about on the waves of time—
present pain alone is absolute.
Only he who hungered knows,
only he who hungered, not a day,
not a year, not two years,
but thirty years, fifty years,
ever since he was old enough to know,
only he knows who looked
into the hollow eye-sockets of his daughters,
he who was gnawed by the sense of shame
and shed wordless tears out of his bones.
Only he knows who wished he could cut
from his bones and flesh to alleviate
the hunger of his loved ones.
Happy are those who are finished;
happy are those who died.

Epilogue, 2

We felt our hearts in March, 1894,
and were amazed at their powerful beating.
We offered them in one offering,
and blood flowed profusely.

In the third month of 1919, once again
we bore witness to our hearts that grew,
bearing arms and washing them in blood,
but blood flowed less.

In the fourth month of 1960, we felt again
the power of our hearts and marched

into the field of history and won,
and lost, but blood flowed little.

Why?
I believe the day of peace will come
bloodless, won by our long-suffering wisdom
and our long-growing compassion,
not to be lost again to blood-suckers.

There will break a new day
when a revolution will come and plant
love and brotherly exchange of labor.

In the dark of winter spring is conceived,
in the dark of our hearts love is conceived.
A revolution will gush forth
like a fountain from every heart.

Then fare thee well.
We will meet again.
As we walk along the ruined walls
our eyebeams may cross.

Know, then, that our meeting is truly
a moment of miracle prepared
by karma through ten kalpas.
If, returning home by a late bus,
I should step on your feet,
forgive me.

Fare thee well.
We may meet with sweet breath
on the paths among rice-paddies,
on the twilit road by the Western Sea
among the ripening millet stalks,
in a sweet encounter.

Fare thee well.

SPRING COMES

Spring comes,
not from the South Seas
nor from the North.

Spring comes, smiling, inclusive,
from the wet paddies and dry fields
between Cheju and the Tumen.

The winter brought mad snowstorms
from the sea and lands
far beyond our land.

Spring comes, all-nourishing,
from within us, from our hearts,
from the villages of this land.

Snow will dissolve
the hardware of hate
that covers the rivers and mountains now.

DRUNKEN SLEEP

Last night as I slept drunken,
I dreamed a funny dream.
I was a butterfly flying up and up.
From above I saw
a peninsula in Asia,
a beautiful land
lapped by foaming seas
on its three sides.
I looked down at its middle,
a zone spreading from Kaesŏng
to the Diamond Mountains,
a girdle four kilometers wide,
demilitarized, beyond forces and arms,
north or south.
I looked at this strip of land,
this lone field of peace.
Last night as I slept drunken,
I dreamed a funny dream.
I saw the demilitarized zone
with its badgers, bear, deer,
their young, and men and their young,
all romping naked and free.
I saw this zone widen and widen
as if by some strange magic,
and I saw tanks that had stood
facing each other across the neutral zone
turn about and retreat
like beetles scattering,
one group beyond Sŏgwip'o
and the other beyond the Tumen.
I saw them throw away their arms
beyond the seas and beyond the sky;
and now the flowering peninsula was
a neutral zone from south to north;

all the hardware was cleared away,
only love breaking new everywhere,
neutrality gushing everywhere,
in the villages of Suni and Tori
reaping a golden harvest.
Last night as I slept drunken,
I dreamed a funny dream.

SHIN KYŎNG-NIM ⑦ 1936-

Translated by David R. McCann and Peter H. Lee

THE WAY HOME (P.L.)

FLOWER SHADOW

MARKET'S CLOSING

THAT DAY

TODAY (P.L.)

FARMER'S DANCE

COUNTRY BUS STATION

WIND (P.L.)

Shin Kyŏng-nim

Born in Chungwŏn, South Ch'ungch'ŏng, on April 6, 1936, Shin Kyŏng-nim was graduated in English literature from Tongguk University (1960). He made his literary debut in 1955 and worked in a number of publishing houses. After a brief unproductive period, he started writing again in the mid-'60s. His subsequent works have shown true affection for the life of the farmer, not a patronizing affection but, as he put it, one directly related to the writer's own historical consciousness. Having suffered at first hand the pangs of social misery and conscious of his roots, Shin views agrarian life with the penetrating eye of a modern man, taking as his own the despair, frustration, and anxiety of the farmer wrestling with the soil. His poems may at first appear to be unremarkable, but they reveal an unobtrusive power of evoking an atmosphere and a mastery of the rhythms of the language, as in "Farmer's Dance," a dance of words resembling the melodic flow of folk music. His first book of poetry, *Farmer's Dance* (1973), won the first Manhae Literary Prize awarded by the influential quarterly *Creation and Criticism*. He also published a collection of critical essays, *Literature and People* (1977).

His poems are seldom impenetrably private or extremely dexterous, but they evince honesty and a warmth of mind and heart. Shin may be a poet of limited scope, but his steadfast dedication to his art, coupled with an indifference to poetic fashion, augurs well for his future work.

P.L.

THE WAY HOME

The whole day without laughter—
Coming home, at the alley tavern
We try to smile but grimace.
When we grasp friendly hands,
They are cold and rough.
We recoil from our haters,
Staggering in dark poverty;
We rage, repent, pledge again—
But then we part.
Shoving open the inner door
Of a hut without a wicker gate,
We call out our wives' names:
But our calls become wails.

FLOWER SHADOW

Where a whiskey bottle and dried squid
were left, on the farm co-op's porch,
the shadow of apricot blossoms.

The wind tugging
at the edge of our clothes
is still cold.
Hunting through newspapers
to find
  PLANT DRY FIELDS

          or

One Percent Less on Farm Taxes

if only our grins
like flowers
          grew bright.

Apricot petal
falling into a whiskey glass.
The co-op's cart
rolling toward market.

MARKET'S CLOSING

We fools are pleased enough
just seeing each other's faces.
Carving a melon by the barber shop,
gulping *makkŏlli* at a wine stall,
we all have old friends' faces.

Talk of drought in the southwest,
of debts to the co-op.

Tapping time with our feet
to the remedy-vendor's guitar,
why do we always
feel such longing for Seoul?

Shall we find some place to play cards?
Tip our wallets
and head for the wine house?

Gathering on the school grounds
we eat pieces of dried squid
and we drink.
                    Gradually
the long summer day ends.
With a pair of rubber shoes
or one salted fish,
down the moon-bright road
the market limps to a close.

THAT DAY

Alone, a young woman
wept, following the bier,
a procession without bells
or funeral banner.
Along the fog-shrouded evening road
phantom shadows.
The wind lifted tree leaves
on a street without doors or windows,
while others watched, hidden
behind phone poles or trees.
No one knew the name
of the one who had died,
that dark day,
with no moon rising.

TODAY

Our bellies full of rice wine
On top of a half-bowl of noodles.
The farmer, foundation of society!
County chief in the lead,
We raise the farmers' banner,
Take a turn round the village head's house.
"We feel the nation's bounty in our hearts."
Gongs and cymbals sound,
The county chief dances a hunchback dance
As the farm advisor beats the drum.
Grain production up 13 to 14 percent!
The expressway's seventy miles away.
Trying to filch dried squid,
Village kids in rags
Knock over a wine jar.
The death of the old man at Dragon Rock
Is no match to soap operas on the radio.
Wives are drunk,
Croaking out their old tunes in the yard;
Girls, within the back fence,
Go hoarse from learning the latest pop-songs.
The whole village drunk and dizzy,
Ah, today, what day is this?
What day?

FARMER'S DANCE

Gong sounded,
curtain lowered.
Makeshift stage, lights
strung from a paulownia.
The viewers have left
an empty playing field.

Faces stained with powder,
we drink, jammed into the wine shop
by the school.
Suffocating, exhausted,
lamentable life.

The cymbal in the lead
we start for the market place,
boys shouting, clinging to us
while young girls cling, giggling,
to the wall of an oil dealer's shop.

The full moon shines as one fellow
bellows like a bandit, another
sneers like Sŏrim the outlaw.
But what use is this commotion,
kicking the heels, crushed
into a hole in the mountains?

Better left to women, this farming
that won't pay
even for the fertilizer.

Past the cow dealers, turning
by the slaughterhouse
comes the spell, and I
lift one foot and blow the brass horn,
shaking my head, twisting my shoulders.

COUNTRY BUS STATION

Once past the sixth block
of Ŭlchiro, downtown,
comes the smells of my country home.

Crossing the muddy yard
of the bus station, into the chill
of the stoveless waiting room,
an old man, ice
dangling from his moustache
—a neighbor, from Sinni Village.
Worried about the rice stacks
still ungathered in his fields
he curses this cold
and the windy snow.
"Oh, is that all you have
for complaints?" some woman
sighs.
        "Is that all
you have for troubles?" adds the mistress
of the wine shop at the crossing.
The waiting room turns colder
as it grows more disordered.
These people from home
are somehow too much for me.
Shall I just leave my seat,
quietly, and take the bus
back to Ŭlchiro, downtown?
Returned to the sixth block, I grow
all the more cowardly.

WIND

You whimper,
   "Grow again, grow again!"
   swinging on a bare branch of an old tree.
You cry,
   tangled in the crushed billboard
   of a seal maker.
You shake the bright window of a beauty parlor;
   spy the bared thighs of young girls
   at play, giggling;
   whirl all the day about the village,
   peeking at a chophouse,
   ducking in and out of a tavern;
   watch a game of *yut* at a rice dealer;
   and passing through the alley,
   search the mudwalled cottages;
   then rattle in a porter's cart,
   descend into the marketplace,
   and amuse yourself
   by the accordion of a blind couple.
You come to sleep when the sun lowers;
   lift the tent of evacuees
   pitched at random on the riverbed
   to find a consumptive old wife;
   go around the theatre;
   arouse the elder daughter, seller of fruits.
   But you cannot melt their despair.
You rummage here and there;
   emerge into the street,
   knocking over the jeweler's signboard,
   covering the cold village with dust;
   then chase the withered leaves into a sewer;
   hurl stones against the windows of the wicked;
   break like waves against the coward's house.

When March comes, you again fool us.
We become you, wind,
milling around the village the whole day.

HWANG TONG-GYU ⓐ 1938-

Translated by Peter H. Lee

Hwang Tong-gyu

Hwang Tong-gyu was born in Seoul on April 9, 1938, the eldest son of a major Korean novelist, Hwang Sun-wŏn, and was graduated in English literature from Seoul National University (1961). After military service (1961–1964), he did graduate work at Seoul National University (1965–1966), received a diploma in English Studies from Edinburgh University (1966–1967), and took part in the International Writing Program at the University of Iowa (1970–1971). Currently he is associate professor of English at Seoul National University. He lives in Seoul with his wife and two children.

His first collection, *One Fine Day* (1961), was followed by *Sad Songs* (1965), two volumes called *The Well-Tempered Clavier* (1968, 1972), published with two fellow-poets, and *Snow Falls in the South* (1974), a volume of new and selected poems. He was also one of the editors of the short-lived magazine of verse, *The Four Seasons (Sagye,* 1966–1968). In 1968 he won a prize from the literary monthly *Contemporary Literature (Hyŏndae munhak).* He also published a collection of critical essays, *The Root of Love* (1976), and has translated T. S. Eliot and Robert Lowell into Korean.

Hwang's early poems reflect his interior journey with its struggles and humiliations. His scope then expands to include the present state of Korea. The country Hwang knows is a country ruled by whims and decrees, where existence is marginal and extinction stalks every man. Bearing testimony to the corruption of justice, the poet determines to live on to express his compassion for humanity, for only the living can endure. Hwang's work, at times dense and elliptical, combines knowledge with terror, honesty with vehemence.

P.L.

FOUR TWILIGHTS

1

Glad omen.
The Chunghŭng monastery is burnt down,
The Taehwa Palace is in ruins.
I balanced a boulder on the cliff
And, looking up day and night,
Trained my eyes.
I can see it.
In June a continuous rain,
In December came long snow.
It's easiest to take life easy;
So easy
I had nights of insomnia.
Glad omen.

2

Irrelevance,
Alternating seasons,
Winds over the spring hills,
The clanking of bells in late autumn.
Inconvenienced,
My ancestors
Fled to the island of Kanghwa.
When winter covered the hills with snow,
Shivering in the cold, I saw sunbeams
In the mouse holes on palace walls.
As I grew older, I made friends
In the dark alleys.
Irrelevance.

3

The wine brewed from yam
Was not sweet on my tongue.
When I grew thin, I had my clothes taken in
And went out, unperturbed, to see a woman
To tell her a long story.
Nothing was easier than deliverance—
Every night I cast off my desire, my skin,
Every morning I found myself
Where I had been the night before.
Every night a dream of shipwreck
Shook me awake at midnight. I drank
Young wine and went back to sleep.
Every morning I remembered the blinding sunlight.

4

Fear assaults me when I walk by the deserted shore.
The girls at South Bank swear
That I'm not yet an old man.
But I'm afraid I may want to die.
My debts being small, my death
Won't make anybody sad.
Hands in pockets,
I watch the drunken sailors scuffle
Under blossoming clouds. I sit
On a deserted boat and smoke.
I'm afraid of the sea at dusk,
Though I know nothing about hell.
Darkness seeps into me before swallowing the sea.

PORT OF CALL

I reached the port on foot.
A long wind from cold places
Shook the houses by the sea;
The lights crept lower and lower,
The sky threatened a long snow.
I crumpled the paper bills with ugly pictures
Into my pocket.
I stubbed out the half-burned cigarette like my shadow
And went down to the shore,
My mind at peace.
The dark hulls creaked in the winds,
Craning their necks to see the port.
Two or three gulls went chasing
Snowflakes in the darkening sky.

SONG OF PEACE

I'm told
We are a puny race.
Doors locked even in daytime,
Bathing our eyes with Trust Drops,
We read essays, hugging the stove.

Dragging the anguish of no place to hide
Like a common soldier,
Travel the country from Kimhae to Hwach'ŏn,
Winter fatigues hanging on you,
A canteen flapping at your side,

Wherever you turn, barbed wire;
Wherever you turn, checkpoints.
I do not understand this love,
This smothering jealous love.

I spread my gloved hands, palms up.
Snow falling for some time now,
A snow colder than snow.

FLIGHT

After ranks and titles vanished,
Dusk over the stationless hills and waters—
Over a nameless night pass,
As a frail pulse rushes away,
So I run away, run away, ever in flight.

Saint-Simon, fever, money scattered
Like fallen leaves,
Standing like a leafless tree,
Looking up at the uncommon moon,
Even cold fades from the numbed senses.

I'll escape to a world—
Where all shining hopes are crushed,
To your suffering,
Your dry coughs,
Lonely men gazing at the moon after midnight,
To the contradictions opposing sleep—
Like a nail driven into a plank, iron shuddering with pain.

WILD GEESE

At the upper reaches of the northern Han
I was not just sad
Seeing all the field cannons march
Down the snow-drifted valleys.

Wild geese came flying low.
I slept and awoke to find myself
Looking through field glasses instead of dreams.

It was a winter of five months
With a few geese here and there.
I saw them strut with their breasts high;
No, they were making love.
A frightening view with a cartridge-belt at my waist.
I wept, laughed, and was reprimanded.

But a new dream came, a dream
Of uncharted land,
The guns made love with their barrels jumping high.
I dreamed in spite of all
And waited and waited fearlessly,
Forgetting dog-tags, frost-bite, even my life.

NOTES OF A KING

FIRST LEAF

The king is but the shade for his subjects.
When you, my lords, raise me
As I kneel below the throne,
And lead me through the back garden
Full of peonies,
I will not look at
The morning or evening papers
Or the telescopes
But will roam among the lonely flowers.

The king should have the grace to depart,
Like the chief of a tribe and his sons
Who burn themselves in a lean year,
Who shout without a cry,
He should learn how to leave,
No cough, no ills, no thatched huts

SECOND LEAF

I have forgotten at what leaf of the winds,
But it was at the dying out of sunset
I smoothed away some sand on an unknown beach
And knelt down with trembling knees.
I saw the minute islands disappear
Netted by the curved horizon.
Who will remember
My endless kneeling in solitude
Throughout this short evening?
Who will remember
The lights carefully put out
In this small land?
From the north to south
The candles nurse the dark in small barracks.
Out there the sea barks slowly without a moon,

With the long waves of our longing.
The wind blows from four quarters.

The wind blows.
The islands are slowly sinking
Beyond our memory.
And this land!
Who will remember
These days of no light
Without even "we" to guard us in our tribulations?
Who will remember
The non-ruins where the non-castle was torn down,
The lightless night with its back toward infinity?

No unhappiness, no life.
Surely there will be a time
When some one will remember them,
The wishes suspended over our twists and turns?
In the dark sky burning clouds
Fall here and there.
Darkness comes to every corner.
Kneeling, I want to fall
Like a lump of clay during the thaw
And float along the east sea, the south sea, the west sea,
And be caught somewhere,
My body changed into their ecstasy.
The wind blows.

SNOW FALLS IN THE SOUTH

Pongjun is weeping, illiterate, illiterate,
Utterly illiterate.
If only he knew how to read the classics,
If only he knew how to cry softly!
Greater kings behind the king,
And now the kings' whip!
Under the winter fog
Horse and foot cross the border again
Without horse-warrants,
The earth cracks like the ribs of a fan,
Guns bawl like lusty children.
If he'd known he would end up
Rubbing his cheeks with cold snow,
He would have gone to Mt. Kyeryong
To till a field,
Till with a sturdy Chinese or Japanese plow.
Snow is falling on the stone bridge
We cross unthinking,
And on the gloomy thatched huts
Where our fathers suffer from a hidden disease.
Listen, snow is falling, unfeeling,
From the leaden sky,
Illiterate, illiterate.

HŎ KYUN, I

Another autumn!
This mountain does not want to change colors.
Vees of geese fly up,
Feathers dishevelled,
Out of your sorrow.
Another mad storm is on the way.
The story's pages drenched with tears,
The hero is killed once more.

At the heart of the city,
The mouse-faced and tiger-eyed
Without a slip,
Without a joke, without even a sign of their presence
Stamp the seal and make a promise
To meet you for the last time.

Open the door and look out.
All is quiet for a moment.
No ancient court, no Yuk Island, no you or I,
Not even sorrow,
Only clouds screened by the moonlight.
A dog you won't find in books
Dares to walk in the open.

HŎ KYUN, II

Who explicates
Complicates
Death.

Look at
Passers-by,
Students with stones in their hands;
Flowers leaning against a wall,
Toppling, spill flower water on the pavement.
Your death is simple.

Simple as a darkening wall
When you put out the light and shut the door.
Your life disappears from the wall:
A drape loosens
And falls to the floor.

Outside snow falls in silence.
It piles up.
It is caressed by anonymous hands—
Trembling hands.
I cannot caress your death.

LIPS

1

A rock suspended above a rock.
Sitting on the rock,
A purple-beaked bird is crying,
A profile of the sky
Pecked by its sharp beak.

2

Two flowers are dying,
Lips of death far lighter
Than our thinking of death alone.
Flowers are gone
And we'll see in the wind our faces.

3

Behind you nobody.
We've been speaking without a voice,
We've been weeping without a sound
For a peace lower than Mt. Samgak,
For the peace of a small valley.
This autumn, tiny insects cry in the wind.
They are there
Blown by the wind.
We are reflected in their eyes
One by one.

4

Scissors! rock! paper!
Scissors! rock! paper!
Snow is coming down on the paper,
A hand
That cannot be clenched into a fist—

A white scream from the children.

276   *Hwang Tong-gyu*

Children are hiding.
Seek them out, they are hiding.
They have not come back from hide-and-seek,
They are hiding, gagged.

SNOW UNDER MARTIAL LAW

Ah, those are sick words.
My soles shiver.
I'm determined to become a simple man!
When dry winds,
Daylong,
Chase the snow here and there,
In the evening
Every snowflake is muddy—
With the sun-shaped sun suddenly down,
My dream shattered,
Prostrate on the ground,
I wipe away my eyes, nose, and mouth.
Terrifying even to myself,
Am I turning into
Muddy snow
Driven about and trampled again?

SONG OF CH'U

I am growing frightened. I can only see the inside of things. In the river bearing torn grasses, fleshless fish frolic, and from the clouds that blossom and fade on the river only a cryptogram flashes. No use trying to decipher it. Tongueless flowers raise their heads and watch the unhappy bodies standing without fear. You may try to get away but you'll shiver with cold. See the fine nets cast everywhere. Ecstatically frightening. I'm not afraid of losing my senses, nor am I afraid of floating like puffs of cloud, sane.

A SMALL STONE

Have you seen a big stone strike
and smash a small stone? Have you
seen other mind-shaken stones hesitate
and avert their eyes? At evening when
the hot light fades and the aching
stones cool, exposing their backs, have
you seen a stone jump by itself into
the water? At the moment when startled
birds fly towards the water's edge,
tangled roads unravel, and darkness
falls, have you seen a stone, not
clinging anywhere, jump unseen into
the water?

AT THE GRAVE OF KIM SU-YŎNG

1

Trees roll up their blinds.
A tedious soft autumn rain
Falls, falls and drenches
The evening glow.

I stand my umbrella against the gravestone,
Lay my wet mind for a while
Down on the ground.
Nothing more to hold on to,
I lean against the sound of rain,
Rubbing my back against the rain.

Is there wind in the sound of rain?
I see the grass trembling.
The leaves of the trees tremble,
The branches tremble,
You tremble clenching your teeth,
Lastly the grass trembles again.

The uprooted does not tremble.

2

Mountains around Seoul are all frozen,
Your mound pushed aside to a corner.
The sky darkens,
The last words relax one by one:
Fall like snowflakes
Light on my head and shoulders,
The back of my hands, my mind.

I'd like to cast out the self,
Only cold flesh remaining, its cold whip—
From the four quarters snowflakes multiply,
One, two, ten, another ten,
They linger in the air,
Then each lifts its head and turns into a white bird,
A white-clawed white bird.

I see a strange light glimmering.
Horizon the span of a hand,
Frozen feet trample on the rest,
It's easy to erase that streak,
Lonely children will erase it unawares—
On this hill the white birds
Turn off the light and fall as snowflakes.

THE ROOT OF LOVE

1
My hometown is
where you walked alone
your hometown is
where I was beaten, spellbound.

Our hometown sleeps
our beaters sleep too
winter has come
old ships are beached.

Taking off hometown and face
we're left only with dance
the sea swells suddenly
ships peel away rust, dripping with sweat.

2
Now love is nothing
love, in that incredibly cloudy day
evening with snow burying the streets
streets blocked by cars, darkly,
bending the joints by the imprisoned taxi
clutching the jumping mighty engine
wheels at your side
running with long strides
sidestepping left and right
love, lift your arms
let's bring out our drawers
suck at the abandoned veins
pierce the dark clouds
and float into the air—
the suppressed dance starts—
Now love is nothing.

3
We're lovely children
we're lovely
lovely children

ah lovely
we're open

the trees standing neatly by the window
they too are busy—
after groping under the earth
they hold their breath for a moment
and touch each other's roots.
Ah lovely

We're lovely children
lovely.

4
Bending its back
a stone edges the snow
and bites a stone.
The bitten stone
laughs brightly.
A wind stops, unwavering.
The moon hangs vast.

Even the forgotten stars gather and glitter—
Now, love is nothing.

WHEN I SEE A WHEEL

When I see a wheel I'd like to roll it.
A bicycle, stroller, rear-car, carriage—
I'd like to roll the wheels that turn.
When I go up a breathtaking slope,
I'd like to roll the wheels of a car.

I can't see things the road holds:
I can. I can't see
My childhood I want to tear down:
I can. I can't see
The girding groves cheeping with birds:
I can. I can't see
The panting republic:
I can. I'd like to roll it.
The piled tangerines in a street stall,
The jars upside-down in a pottery shop,
The men lying arched,
I'd like to roll everything once
Before it falls
On the path of birds.

CHŎNG HYŎN-JONG ⑦ 1939-

Translated by U-ch'ang Kim

Chŏng Hyŏn-jong

Chŏng Hyŏn-jong was born in Seoul on December 17, 1939, and was graduated in philosophy from Yonsei University (1964). From October 1974 to March 1975 he took part in the International Writing Program at the University of Iowa. He has held a number of editorial jobs and is now a professor of creative writing at the Seoul College of Arts. He is married and has one son. He made his literary debut in 1964, published his first collection, *The Dream of Things*, in 1972, most of which is contained in *The Festival of Pain*, his second book (1974), and he has translated Yeats and Frost into Korean.

Chŏng has been concerned with the epistemological exploration of the relation of the imagination and its varied objects, and he may be termed a philosophical poet for his generalized abstract attitude toward his subjects, his wit, his ability to make satirical synopses of certain situations, and his absurdist humor. His poetry shows an anguished perception of the groundlessness of human existence that emanates from the ordeals of the war-torn years. The nihilistic despair of the war years is, however, modulated into a quieter recognition of the futility of the repetitive humdrum existence of modern man. Unlike others, he maintains a humorous distance from his own acceptance of the existential appraisal of the human situation. More often, his theme concerns the possibility of happiness in the untoward occasions of life, as one of his characteristic figures, the rainbow formed by waterdrops high in the air, suggests. Given the political atmosphere of Korea since the late '60s, his sense of happiness has become a commitment to the ideal of freedom. Although his perception of life is philosophically gloomy, in his engagement with life—lively and optimistic—he is indeed a "festivalist of pain."

U.K.

WATERDROPS OF THE RAINBOW LAND

Waterdrops, drunk with the sun,
put on the brightest colors
high up in midair. They forget
the fate that will pull them down,
just as we dwell on earth, forgetting
the fate that will pull us down
to the lowest dark of the earth.
Waterdrops, drunk with their beauty,
with love, recklessness, alcohol,
the surge of the racing blood,
and with follies and time—
they hang in midair
between the heat of devils
and the heat of angels: waterdrops,
shining vapors of the rainbow land.

A WALK

The mind of water comes
and freezes water. The stars shine
in the wistfulness of the mind.
The wind blows. I am out walking
with a mind of sand.

Melancholy sinks into the marrow;
desire comes whispering;
consciousness burns like fire.
Among these, incredibly, I want
to play, to practice. Therefore,
I am out walking in the spring night.

The air worried in the day is now
a bridge from stillness to stillness.
The air by street lights is by street lights;
the air by the tree is by the tree;
now things flow in their own color
and in their own rhythm. Yet we are out
far from home with the wind at night;
lights and longing are out
where there is no peace.

CORRESPONDENCES

The street lights that night lights,
like its heart within,
and the fog that lets the street lights
flow, warm and red in the night.

The tongue of the damp fog,
the vacant tongue of street lights
breathing the minutest tremor
of each other's sound,
tears and desire mingling.

BRIGHT SLEEP

His sleep weeps often,
insinuating into all that wanders,
the loneliness of a yawning man,
the road one takes inside the pocket,
and it answers to the voice of time
asking, "How do you like repetition?"
in the gurgles of tea as it is poured
from the kettle into the cups.
Sleep comes with no determination thereunto,
but death is the sleep of the sea waves
which have nothing to rest upon.

His sleep weeps often
as night locks its gates deeply.
On night's gates, starlight knocks
sending off bright sparks.
One morning wakes up another morning,
mornings awakening each other,
cleanly and brightly darting
their bright morning beams.
Sleep wakes up, weeping a little
like a song that hums by itself
without our determination thereunto.

MATTER THAT IS SHAMELESS

Endless matter coyly reveals death;
matter, intense and hard, remembers death.
My ears are brightly touched,
my eyes are dizzyingly whorled
by the winding labyrinth of matter
which tries hard to desire nothing,
shameless and hard.

ARE YOU STARS?
—TO THE POETS

Stars like the stars in the sky,
sands like the sands by the sea.
That which shines shines,
that which is alone is alone.
Until you can sing, "I am
the one that shines in the shining
of that which shines," wait.
Until your body is heavy night
over the desert and the sand
and the wind blowing over the sand,
play, practice. And love
your untruth until your untruth
ceases to be untruth.

HER WEEPING PASSES BY MY EARS AND RESTS EVER IN THE KINGDOM OF WEEPING

I wish she would not weep
even when she is by herself.
I wish I wouldn't have to think
about her weeping when I am alone.
Her weeping is always hers,
a kingdom of her own.
I know this, but my ears are lovely
when they hear her weeping alone.

THE DREAM OF THINGS

1. The Dream of the Tree

The dream dreams its power,
as it kisses the sunlight
streaming on its leaves.
The tree dreams its blood
and speaks, rubbing its cheeks
against the falling rain.
The tree hears its life shaking
as the wind's green power
shakes its branches.

THE ABYSS OF SOUND

1. Sound Longs for the Ear

I peel the skin of sound:
it doesn't take too long.
Sound knows the ear, love-deepened,
and steals the ear to shape it for itself
as an ear attached to sound.
Sound listens to sound's voice,
shaking my whole body, now an ear.
Death coils in the heart of sound;
sound longs for sound's ear.

2. A Bright-tempered Man

Why is my temper so bright?
Do you see how the sun walks
until day gathers its tail, sun-colored,
and hides in the night? Oh, me—
how bright-tempered, dizzily bright.

To choke the throat of high noon,
I walk to the sea of meals,
I walk to the sea of soup,
carefully taking daily bread
and nothing else. But even then
daily pleasure tempts me, nailing down
my wings, with the hammer of feet,
the hammer of laughter and tears.
O, bright, bright-tempered me,
dizzily bright.

Chŏng Hyŏn-jong   297

It is possible to go up and down
the steps of the clear air of noon,
but all sound is lonely, as you well know.
Say that the blue eye of the sad wind
watches the sound of the wind,
which I hold in my hands, not knowing
what to do with what I hold.

3. The Hole of Sound

The form of a man goes away,
leaving a body-shaped hole;
the form of a woman goes away
leaving a body-shaped hole
in the air cut by her body.
The air keeps these holes.
My senses are closed to the world.
The hole tempts me where sound made it
in the air—form fixed by sound,
the lonely mode of its being.
One walks down the steps,
the darker, the better for memory.
Sound and its hold are sharper-edged
in the dark; they hurt more
than the sound of the air
unstained by this darkness.
(Where are they, the sound-owners,
wrapped in love and tears?)

4. Soundless

I see a heap of stillness,
lying blood-smeared;
this stillness was once light,
stillness, comrade of sound.

I see a heap of stillness,
blood-smeared.
Word bites the tail of soundless;
soundless the tail of word,
each waiting to strike
like mortal enemies.

TO THE ACTORS

Throw away acting;
nothing is for keeps.
Throw away speech.
Have you thrown away?
Throw away when you've thrown away.
Throw it away when it is yours.
Throw away yourself.
Throw away applause.

Laugh the laughter being thrown away;
express the expression being thrown away.
Let sorrow belong to sorrow,
let action belong to action,
let speech belong to speech,
let each belong to each.
Then peace may be with you
even if sorrow stays,
even if death gives back
action and speech . . .
then, and yet,
then, and yet . . .

POETRY, IDLE POETRY

What can you love with poetry?
What can you mourn with poetry?
What can you get and what can you lose?
What can you set up and what can you pull down?
If you cannot love death with death,
If you cannot love life with life,
If you cannot grieve with grief,
If you cannot love poetry with poetry,
what then can you love with poetry?

No one sees the snow that falls at night;
no one walks on it, no footsteps.
It is: silent, clear,
beautiful by itself.

Chŏng Hyŏn-jong   301

THE FESTIVAL OF PAIN, I

1. A Letter

The seasons change. If you know the occasions of life,
I love you. Occasions? What big occasions! I love you.
When I see you, the world colors my senses. Color is the
void, the void color. Life hangs between color and the void.
We say, it is color, and we say, it is void; but it is the reality
of things in this world. Just to think of it, I choke on
the thought. When I see you, I become colors, I become void.
The letters we write are the brotherhood of our feelings, our
secret channels. Thus I write a letter to you.

A ball of fire burns in the air, looking like a man thinking;
a ball of tears burns in the air, looking like citizens.
Tears wet the fire, and the ball of fire burns. The bonfire of
    flames
and tears shoots up in the air and becomes the shape of the
    people
of this country: a ball of blood burning in the black night sky.
"An age passes and an age comes," sings a chorus, circling
around the deep silence of the night.

I do not want to write in chained words. Chained words tell
of things in chains. I want to write my letter in words
that cannot be chained. For ever and ever. I am a festivalist—
the festivalist of pain, which is, of all festivals, the most
brilliant. A chorus sings, "We are happy." I love you, you who
know the occasions of life. Peace and happiness to you.

THE FESTIVAL OF PAIN, II

Blinking, shining stars,
Look at the chorus of burning cigarettes
in the constellation of Sagittarius!
Hear in the dark night of slogans
the long music of our passwords!
I give the sky wholly to the birds
and fly downwards to the earth.
    Pleasure binds the bodies;
    pain binds the souls.

We wanted to pluck the roots of time;
it is we, instead, that are plucked.
Sorrow of things, beauty of things!
Wine flows, shining adjective of the spirit.
The song in our eyes harks back to home.
    Pleasure binds the bodies;
    pain binds the souls.

What keeps us in life? The power
of the miscellanies of the mind!
The blue sky of folk songs weeps today,
clear and blue. Care falls over the stars
and beggars us, cowed, wandering souls.
    Pleasure binds the bodies;
    pain binds the souls.

The shadow is heavier than the body;
we walk, therefore, hanging our heads
and sing of the things of man,
adding salt to blood, sugar to tears.
To love man is the loneliest thing of all.
    Pleasure binds the bodies;
    pain binds the souls.

Chŏng Hyŏn-jong   303

THINGS FLOATING IN THE AIR

1. A Stone

In midair floats
a stone projectile
rumored by some to be political.

The rumor is a fossil,
its age unknown. It is a fate.
It is known that it is not comical.

We live from hand to mouth
on iron propaganda,
the daily ration of poisoned food.

2. Me or Self-Identity

If I become heavier by day,
it is because of fear.

I run and run
away from my shadow.

I tear it off with my hands
because I fear another shadow.

A substance without shadow
speaks, floating in midair,

I am not me,
I am not me.

3. The Mirror

Mirrors
mirroring meaningful acts are
almost shattered.

A giant mirror
hangs in midair with the legend:
Blessed are the lowly.

Happy are those who lie low.
This is the Sŏn wisdom
distilled by the age.

The mirror shows:
the low-lying, the sleeping
and those who are dead.

It is the only way
of looking at oneself
the age permits.

Home is the closed eye;
a land of exile is
the eye that stays open.

4. Home

There are holes in every roof.
They are for sticking
one's hands through.
How convenient!

Lest rain come through
keep your hands up,
the loudspeaker announces.
How kindly!

Stars are many in the sky.
What is my home like?
A ferryboat? A freighter?
A patrol boat?

Moon, moon, bright moon!
Let me build a house on the smoke
and live a thousand years,
ten thousand years!

A PAINFUL HISTORY: AN OUTLINE

Once upon a time there lived Trap and Snare. Trap tried
to trap Snare, and Snare tried to snare Trap.
      Only stones lived.
      Only iron lived.
      We? We were stones within stones,
      We were iron within iron.
One day Trap trapped Snare, and Snare snared Trap.
And then Trap and Snare fell to a pitfall.

WAR

It justifies my life, the tryst of fear and fear, sleeptalk between iron meals. It justifies unity of thought, unity of will, unity of feelings. It justifies cowardice, contempt, fear, frustration, paralysis, freedom springing back from paralysis. It justifies the sulfurous air, a hundred percent happiness promised by the loudspeaker silken-smooth, generous like water or fire.

> My work is only one—
> to dance, like the wind
> embracing the grass,
> like the wind jumping into arms,
> to dance, quietly, quietly.

O MOON, THE SOURCE OF MORALITY

A piece of wind lies
fallen on the sandy road.
I pick it up. I feel it
and hear it with my ears
like the sound of the moonrise.

O moon, the source of morality,
and the sea waves, another source!
My laughter surges like the waves
in the eye where the moon rises.

KIM CHI-HA ⟨ℤ⟩ 1941-

Translated by David R. McCann

NO ONE

BY THE SEA

TWO A.M.

YELLOW EARTH ROAD

JANUARY 1974

A SMILE

THE STORY OF A SOUND (FROM ''GROUNDLESS RUMORS'')

Kim Chi-ha

Kim Chi-ha, born in 1941, has passed most of the last six years in prison. He has been sentenced to death, then life, then another twenty-six years for writing and publishing a number of satirical poems, for his activities in support of critics of the South Korean regime, and most recently for the thoughts expressed in his prison journals and implied by the books he owns. He is in all senses of the term a political prisoner.

Kim is also a gifted poet, one who has made his art serve his life. In the course of his growth as a poet, he has moved from the distant, impersonal tone of such poems as "No One," taken from *Yellow Earth* (1972), the only collection of his poems to be published in Korea, to the openness of "By the Sea" and "Two A.M.," among those which circulated in *samidzat* form in 1974, while he was "hiding" from the authorities. He has also explored the rich resources of traditional Korean oral literature in the long satirical poems that constitute the middle portion of his career. The excerpt from "Story of a Sound," selected in turn from the long poem "Groundless Rumors," illustrates Kim's use of the narrative style and irreverent tone of the folk dramas.

In a happier time, Kim Chi-ha's efforts to adapt traditional Korean verse forms and oral genres to a modern outlook would be more generally apprehended than present conditions in the Korean literary world allow. As it is, Kim Chi-ha's poems cannot be separated from his life, and his life cannot be seen apart from the present social and political conditions of life in South Korea.

D.M.

NO ONE

From here
all the way there
no one at all.

Above a black
stream, on a stone
bridge where moonlight collapses,
in this strangely beautiful house,
cloudy with breath,
no one at all.

Dark,
the midst of an old dream
of my twisted limbs crushed
by the coin rolling
round in the moon
              is dark,

and on the road running
away from me
           dying
in blue-dyed brain,
no one at all.

BY THE SEA

Snow is falling.
I drink cheap whiskey
and chew the tears
that fall on the dried fish.
I chew the sighs
within my fearful heart, my gestures,
and each path in secret I have come down.

I am alone—
In this last space, an edge
too small for a pin
I am alone,
my friends.

I pour whiskey
over the old memories of the chains
that have scored my wrists,
and leaning against the anger
that rises from such memories
I reach out for your faces,
one by one.

I will not flow out.
Where blizzards whirl over the sea
I will not go out.
Even with an inch less
than an inch of earth,
and bound to this wretched edge
I will return,
my friends.

To the furrows scored
by the painful labor of strong wrists
—not to chains, not chains—
and to your faces, your pain
I will return, my friends.

Hidden and alone
I will be reborn by the snow-lashed sea.
Rending this mad heart,
tearing it open
I cry out like a child.
I will return.

TWO A.M.

2:00 A.M. is the middle hour.
Unable to sleep, to splash my face with cold water,
to read a book.
Too exhausted to daydream,
no inclination to get up and walk.
Unable to eat, in sorrow for my neighbors;
too embarrassed even to mutter
something to myself. Unable
to sit still.

Unable to do anything.
2:00 A.M.
The middle hour,
this age.

YELLOW EARTH ROAD

Down the road through the yellow earth
I follow the fallen drops
of blood, Father.
Where you died
           now blackened
only the sun burns.

Sweat, tears, and the barley-scorching
sun.
    Out into the heat,
Father, under the bayonets and the gun muzzles
I am going to the place where you died
in a rice sack, as mullet leaped
and twisted, by the side
of Oldfather Creek.

Each night the beacon fires rose on Op'o Mountain,
till one day light fell on the land,
over this yellow earth
                  insistent as the force which drives
renewal to the hedgerow oranges, to the single inner leaf
green as the salt sea water.
Let us shout out the rallying cries
      which gleamed bright as day;
Sing out the songs of that day.

In Hwadang, where the bamboo grows
round about in scrawny knots,
blood rises in all the wells
every ten years:
           Father
born on this barren, colonized soil,

and felled by the guns and bayonets.
In the water droplets
forming on the young bamboo shoots
I come to know May, clear as crystal.

Then the long, cruel summer
when even the smallest infants were starving;
the hot summer of unbounded tyranny,
reaching, at the very end,
to all the ways of this land,
the yellow earth road,
our hopes.

Climbing the beach path where decrepit boats
rot apart in the sun,
crossing the pale white furrows
of the buckwheat fields
to whirl against the lofty skies,
those shouts and cries are now
ten years past.

Sensing your voice again
in this breath and flesh bound with wire,
Father, I am going to the place by the creek
where mullet leap and turn, to the place
where you died in a rice sack.

JANUARY 1974

January 1974—call it death.

The light extinguished from your eyes
at the announcement that afternoon on the street—

Call it death.

That moment the blood frozen within your cold,
constricted heart
    burst out, flowing hot and strong again,
the blizzards swept back in—
                              Call it death.

When the others had all been dragged off, leaving you
awkwardly alone, and you had hidden yourself
away by the distant sea,

in the dim corner of a mirror
on some unfamiliar wine house wall,
some wretch's fear-worn face, his back
split by the knife of this dark age—
Call the lines of weariness on his face,
call them death.

After so much
hardship, that day love began,
that cold, windy day I first took your hand
and for the first time overcoming my fears
looked at your face
directly, that day
of parting from you—
                      Call it death.

Kim Chi-ha   319

This heart that will not believe
that even on one cold, wind-swept street
the unleashed petals would burst
with great cry through the late chill
of impending spring—
                    Call it death.

And if not suspecting, disbelieving,
then all the fearful, anxious expressions—
                    Call these death.

Calling it
death, January 1974,
we shall name it betrayal.

Let us shake our whole being,
shake our whole being
and refuse it,

till memory
of the last warm drop of sweat
in your hand
and mine
grows cold.

A SMILE

Awakening
in the dew with a full shout awakening,
pressing down the grasses,
white in the dawn's luster,
pressing them down
I went on, forgetting all that lay
beneath my steps and far behind me.

I shouldered the weight of a heart's remorse
and took flight.
As mountain ridges turned and twisted
in that shout, that far-away city
dawn returned at last
in the blood-shot eyes
of friends, through the beatings
in the rusted cells,
through that desolate freedom

as the dew moistened my warm forehead.

Ah, but then I was standing,
and the grasses, left forgotten
beneath my steps and far behind me
arose, burning white as the spirit
of the summer earth.
Bluffs, valleys, ridges—all rose up,
like a battle-cry, like fire
rose up in ecstasy.

Then for the first time I learned that smile
and knew the meaning of history:
the hot summer of my twenty-third year,
a season of such simplicity.

THE STORY OF A SOUND
(FROM "GROUNDLESS RUMORS")

It wasn't in Russia, China, Japan,
or America either, but here in Korea,
the eastern part of Seoul,
where the dust swarms up in Ch'ŏngyangni,
and beyond it lie the coal-black fluids
of Chungnang Brook.
Jammed together down its banks,
the squatter shacks perch in bunches wherever they fit,
rattling this way, trembling that
in the slightest breeze blowing by.
Way in the back of the darkest corner
of the most ramshackle shack
lived Ando, up from the country
to find his fortune.

Ando worked like an ox,
but was timid as a mouse, simple
as a sheep—the harmless sort
who doesn't need laws to live right.
But some strange twist of fate,
some lousy inheritance from a previous life
made whatever he tried
                              go bad.
It might start well, but it wouldn't come out;
what looked good for a while just wouldn't turn out.

Get married?
                    How could he? He couldn't find a girl friend.
Buy a house?
                    Not a chance. He couldn't get the rent for a whole
                    room.
He couldn't find money for food, and if it looked
like he might get a job, well,

from this day to that day to the very next day
they kept putting him off till it went up in smoke.

"No backer? No go here."
                              "No school tie? Nothing doing."
"No deposit? No return."
                    "No soup? No dessert."

Without any money, and no one to help,
there wasn't a deal he could start.
The shake-down artists shook him,
the rake-off operators raked him,
till not a thing was left.
He could yell all he pleased—it was no use.
Or fling himself down in a rage—no help.
He could struggle, kick, open his eyes wide
and glare all around, or just close them,
resigned to his fate:
                              it made no difference,
it was all the same, and no good.

He began to think of hanging himself,
but couldn't find a rafter.
Gas wouldn't do—the windows were full of holes.
He couldn't slip away
on a mixture of poison and wine—
there was no money for a cup
and nothing else to use,
so no way, he had no way:
no way to resist, no way to protest;
no way to rest, no way to put his feet
down on the ground and just stand.

Just once to have the guts
to stand up firm on his own two feet
would have brought down a flood of accusations
for crimes never heard of before, never seen, never imagined.

Notes

INTRODUCTION

Childe Harold's Pilgrimage: canto 4, 181–184.

Mallarmé: from "Réponses à des enquêtes sur l'évolution littéraire," *Oeuvres Complètes* (Paris: Gallimard, 1945), p. 869. Translation from Bradford Cook, *Mallarmé: Selected Prose Poems, Essays, and Letters* (Baltimore: Johns Hopkins University Press, 1956), p. 21.

Verlaine: "Never the Color, always the Shade, / always the nuance is supreme!" C. F. MacIntyre, tr., *French Symbolist Poetry* (Berkeley: University of California Press, 1961), p. 35.

Baudelaire: "perfumes, sounds, and colors correspond." MacIntyre, p. 13.

'spots of time': René Wellek, *A History of Modern Criticism: The Late Nineteenth Century* (New Haven: Yale University Press, 1965), pp. 437.

Esperanto: for example, Verlaine's "Chanson d'automne."

Kim's first volume of new verse: titled *Songs of a Jellyfish*, it comprised 83 pieces, most of which were written in 1922–1923.

Tagore: known to Korea from about 1916; the first group of translations appeared in November 1917, and *The Crescent Moon* and *The Gardener* in 1924.

"The Summons of the Soul": from Peter H. Lee, *Poems from Korea* (Honolulu: University Press of Hawaii, 1974), p. 167.

Yi Sang-hwa: see *Poems from Korea*, pp. 163–164.

Hannah Arendt: The Human Condition (Chicago: University of Chicago Press, 1958), esp. p. 221.

Imagistic: Pound's famous definition of the image appeared in *Poetry*, March 1913.

lucid apprehension of nature: U-chang Kim, "Sorrow and Stillness: A View of Modern Korean Poetry," *Literature East and West*, 13 (June 1969):154.

urban word-guerrillas: a phrase from Laurence Lieberman, *Unassigned Frequencies* (Urbana: University of Illinois Press, 1977), p. 44.

Eliot and Tate: I have in mind Eliot's "The Waste Land" and Tate's "Seasons of the Soul" (1944).

HAN YONG-UN
At the Shrine of Non'gae

Non'gae: a professional female entertainer, d. 1592, was a mistress of the military commander of Chinju during the Hideyoshi invasion. At a banquet in the Ch'oksŏk Tower she jumped into the South River with a Japanese general in her arms.

The Sŏn Master's Sermon

Sŏn: the Korean reading of Ch'an or Zen.

KIM SOWŎL
Samsu Kapsan

This poem was included in Kim's last letter to his mentor, Kim Ŏk, and was published posthumously in the latter's "Remembrance of Kim Sowŏl." Kim Ŏk himself had published a poem under the same title, which told of his longing to return to Samsu Kapsan, a region in the northeastern part of Korea used as a place of exile during the Yi dynasty. "That ancient road to exile" refers to a Chinese region (Shu, modern Szechwan; as in, for example, Li Po's poem "The Road to Shu Is Hard") of similar usage.

YI YUKSA
Dusk

9] *the Twelve Houses:* perhaps referring to the duodenary terms, the 12 Jupiter-stations; see Joseph Needham, *Science and Civilization in China,* III (Cambridge, 1959), 402–404, esp. table 34.

Flower

12] *My mob of memories:* may also refer to his friends.

CHŎNG CHI-YONG
Pomegranate

14] *Silla:* one of the three ancient Korean kingdoms, the traditional dates of which are 57 B.C.–A.D. 935; hence a round number, one thousand.

News of May

2] *Paulownia: odong* in Korean; *wu-t'ung* in Chinese, the tree upon which the phoenix is said to perch, hence some suggest "the phoenix tree." It is often associated with autumn's loneliness and sadness, when its large leaves fall, arousing sorrow in the heart of the beholder.

The T'aegŭk Fan

The fan with a symbol of *t'aegŭk* (Great Ultimate or Absolute), represented by a circle consisting of *S*-divided halves in blue and red colors symbolizing the principles of *yin* and *yang.* The symbol appears in the national flag of the Republic of Korea.

Window, I

Composed on the occasion of his child's illness and subsequent death.

White Deer Lake

A lake in the crater of Mount Halla, on Cheju Island, 600 m from east to west, 500 m from north to south.

11] *ghostly flowers: Toch'ebi* in Korean

17] *ri:* a common Korean measure of distance, about 400 meters.

17] *Sŏgwip'o:* a town in the south of Cheju Island.

19] *a strange mother:* refers to the Japanese colonizers.

YUN TONG-JU
Another Home

9] *A faithful dog:* can also be read ironically as "a foolishly faithful dog," which, unaware of the voice of Heaven or that of the beautiful soul, only makes the sound of darkness. See Kim U-ch'ang, *The Poet in the Age of Need* (Seoul: Minŭmsa, 1977), p. 187.

Counting the Stars

22] *Francis Jammes:* a French poet (1868–1938) whose exquisite treatment of young girls, animals, and objects delighted the reader; *Rainer Maria Rilke* (1875–1926), the author of *Duino Elegies* (1923) and *Sonnets to Orpheus* (1923).

26] *Kando:* Chien-tao in Chinese, the southeastern part of Manchuria, where there were Korean settlements.

SŎ CHŎNG-JU
Postcard: To a Friend

12] *Li Po:* a famous T'ang poet whose dates are 701—762.

My Wife

6] *p'iri:* a reed instrument with a piercing, nasal sound.

Old Fashioned Hours

22] *makkŏlli:* a coarse, fermented rice wine.

PAK TU-JIN
Hyanghyŏn

Hyanghyŏn means "fragrant peak."

Hymn to the Graveyard

7] *Granny-flowers:* in the original, *halmikkot,* a pasqueflower or wind-flower, here translated literally.

7] Onomatopoeia of bird calls *(ppii ppii pae paetchong paetchong)* omitted here.

Mount Tobong

A small mountain near Yangju in Kyŏnggi province, 717 m high.

Soul-Sellers

6] *Gold, silver, . . .:* traditional tributes sent to China by annual Korean missions.

8] *vocal cords:* a metonymy for life.

9] One line has been omitted at this point.

Self-Portrait

31] *Thy Word:* the poet tells me that he intended the trinity, but in translation I have used the singular.

PAK MOGWŎL

At the Center

24] *kalpa:* aeon, age of incalculable time, a fabulous period of time in Buddhism.

KIM SU-YŎNG

The Game in the Moon

23] *ondol:* the Korean under-floor heating system, where a room is floored with flat stones to make a hypocaust.

Do You Know?

5] *Graham:* perhaps Martha Graham.

17] *Paegyang and Arirang cigarettes:* cheaper brands of Korean cigarettes; Arirang was the more expensive of the two.

Walking Out of the Old Palace

3] *50-won:* equivalent to 10 cents in U.S. currency.

KIM CH'UN-SU

The Season of Rain

1] *Nukeia:* a girl's name coined by the poet, who may have had in mind the Korean word *nungnung-hada,* meaning "unpleasantly wet," together with a vague suggestion of a Greek name.

Homecoming

12] *tradition-rich furnaces:* anthracite coal is the main fuel used for heating in Seoul; but some die of carbon monoxide poisoning, especially in the ill-ventilated houses of the poorer classes.

SHIN TONG-YŎP

To Hyang

1] *Hyang:* a girl's name, meaning fragrance.

Keep Your Eyes Clear

The translator has omitted the last stanza.

A Head of Day Lily

14] *bean soup:* fermented bean soup, a favorite in Korea, often taken as a symbol of the country's earthy agrarian tradition.

20] *Three Hans:* ancient tribes in southern Korea who formed three loosely allied tribal states before the Christian era.

March

16] *Cheju:* an island off the peninsula, forming the southernmost tip.

18] *globefish eggs:* considered a delicacy in Korea, the globefish requires careful preparation before it can be eaten because of poison in its intestines. The poor who try to make use of the fish's discarded parts often become poison victims.

23] *Kwanghwamun:* the showcase boulevard in Seoul.

43] *Asanyŏ:* a legendary unhappy lover of Silla, used by Shin to symbolize the people's nationalistic yearning for a unified Korea.

46] *Tonghak:* Eastern Learning, a nativist popular movement of the late nineteenth century. The peasant rebellion inspired by the Eastern Learning, which gathered considerable strength in the southwest, met its final defeat near the Kŭm River in South Ch'ungch'ŏng.

50] *Sobaek Mountains:* a mountain range forming the backbone of the southern part of the peninsula.

Selections from *The Kŭm River*

2] *1960:* the date of the student uprising that toppled Syngman Rhee's government.

12] *1919:* a reference to the Independence Movement of 1919.

13] *1894:* the year of the Tonghak rebellion.

39] *Suun:* the founder of Tonghak, Ch'oe Che-u (1824–1864); Suun is his penname.

76] *Haewŏl:* the second Master of Tonghak, Ch'oe Si-Hyŏng (1829–1898).

105] *T'aebaek Mountains:* a mountain range running through the eastern part of Korea.

Spring Comes

6] *Tumen:* the Tumen River forms a natural border between Korea and China and Soviet Russia.

Drunken Sleep

10] *Kaesŏng:* a city near the Demilitarized Zone on the North Korean side.

11] *Diamond Mountains:* the famous scenic area near the Eastern Sea, now in North Korea.

38] *Suni and Tori:* common Korean names.

SHIN KYŎNG-NIM
Wind

13] *yut:* a popular game played with four round-backed, flat-faced sticks, usually by two sides. The sticks are thrown in the air and the score depends on how they land.

HWANG TONG-GYU
Four Twilights

2] *Chunghŭng monastery:* a temple to the south of Mount Samgak in Seoul, which crumbled in 1915 leaving only the foundation.

3] *Taehwa Palace:* a temporary royal palace built in 1129 near Taedonggun in South P'yŏngan. Only the ruins remain.

20] *island of Kanghwa:* a mountainous island on the west coast off Seoul, a place of refuge for the royal court during the Yi dynasty.

Song of Peace

4] *Trust Drops:* the name of an eye lotion.

8] *Kimhae:* a district in South Kyŏngsang; Hwach'ŏn, a district in the midwest of Kangwŏn province.

Flight

6] *Saint-Simon:* the French reformer (1760–1825) whose writings have been popular among students in Korea in recent decades.

Notes of a King

SECOND LEAF

39] *changed into their ecstasy:* expresses his affection for a small, blocked, and divided country. The protagonist is a king who, floating like "a lump of clay," changes into their [his people's] ecstasy.

Snow Falls in the South

1] *Pongjun:* Chŏn Pong-jun (1854–1895), a Tonghak (Eastern Learning) leader of a peasant rebellion of 1894 in Kobu county in North Chŏlla. The government troops were helpless against the uprising, and subsequently the forces of China and Japan were brought in, which resulted in the Sino-Japanese war.

5] *Greater kings:* the rulers of China and Japan who intervened to quell the Tonghak rebellion in 1894.

9] *horse-warrants: map'ae,* a round badge made of copper, about 10 cm in diameter. On onè side is a picture of one to ten horses, and on the other side the issuing office and the date with a seal. Used by officials to levy horses in the provinces; also used by the Secret Royal Inspector as his identification.

14] *Mt. Kyeryong:* in South Ch'ungch'ŏng, 828 m high, regarded in folk belief as the site of the capital for a millennium.

Hŏ Kyun, I

Hŏ Kyun (1569–1618), author of the *Hong Kiltong chŏn* (Life of Hong Kiltong), a picaresque story. An illegitimate son of Minister Hŏ Yŏp and an active organizer of reform movements, he was captured and executed on a charge of treason. The hero of the story, Hong Kiltong, together with his band of righteous thieves, seizes wealth unjustly exacted by rapacious officials and distributes it among the poor. He then sails off to Yuk Island, where he builds a classless utopia.

20] *A dog:* comparable to "a pig" in the West, says the poet.

Song of Ch'u

A reference to the struggles between Liu Pang, founder of the Han (r. 202–195) and Hsiang Yü, the king of Ch'u (d. 203–202 B.C.). In the night Hsiang Yü heard "the Han armies all about him singing the songs of Ch'u. 'Has Han already conquered Ch'u?' He exclaimed in astonishment." See Burton Watson, *Records of the Grand Historian of China* (New York, 1961), I, 70.

At the Grave of Kim Su-yŏng

18] *erase that streak:* expresses a concern that Kim's life and accomplishments might be easily blotted out and forgotten.

The Root of Love

Two lovers are compared to "ships peeling away rust" in sect. 1. The next section describes the ecstatic state, as if possessed, in which the lovers find themselves.

CHŎNG HYŎN-JONG

The Festival of Pain

3–4] *color is the void, the void color:* all existence is dependent on causation—all things are relative. Color refers to the phenomenal world, often taken to mean sexuality, and void refers to the Buddhist idea that all things of the phenomenal world are illusions.

Festival of Pain, II

8–9] *Pleasure binds the bodies . . . :* the refrain from Miguel de Unamuno's "Love, Pain, Compassion, Personality" (1913): "For to love means to pity, and, though their bodies are united by pleasure, their souls are united by pain." See *The Tragic Sense of Life in Men and Nations,* tr. Anthony Kerrigan, Bollingen Series 85:4 (Princeton, 1972), p. 149.

Select Bibliographies

Books mentioned were published in Seoul, unless stated otherwise.

HAN YONG-UN

Collected Works of Han Yong-un *(Han Yong-un chŏnjip)*. 6 vols. Sin'gu munhwasa, 1973–1974. Volume 1 contains all the poetic works including his *sijo* and poetry in Chinese. However, the basic text remains:
The Silence of Love *(Nim ŭi ch'immuk)*. 1926. Facsimile edition available as number 23 of *Ch'ogan hŭigwi Han'guk hyŏndaesi wŏnbon ch'ŏnjip* (Hoedang sŏgwan, 1970).

KIM SOWŎL

Azaleas *(Chindallaekkot)*. Tongmunsa, 1925.
Selected Poems *(Sowŏl sich'o)*, ed. Kim Ŏk. Pangmun sŏgwan, 1939. Other editions were published in 1956, 1966, 1970, and 1975.

YI YUKSA

Collected Poems *(Yuksa sijip)*. Seoul ch'ulp'ansa, 1946 (reprint, Pŏmjosa, 1956). Also printed as Deep-Purple Grapes *(Ch'ŏngp'odo)*, Pŏmjosa, 1964 and Sŏrim munhwasa, 1977, and The Wide Plain *(Kwangya)*, Hyŏngsŏl ch'ulp'ansa, 1971. The best pocket edition is Collected Works of Yi Yuksa *(Yi Yuksa chŏnjip)*, Chŏngŭm mun'go 70, 1975.

CHŎNG CHI-YONG

Collected Poems *(Chŏng Chi-yong sijip)*. Simunhaksa, 1935; Kŏnsŏl ch'ulp'ansa, 1946.
White Deer Lake *(Paengnoktam)*. Munjangsa, 1941; Paegyangdang, 1946.
Selected Poems *(Chi-yong sisŏn)*. Ŭryu munhwasa, 1946.

YUN TONG-JU

Sky, Wind, Stars, and Poetry *(Hanŭl kwa param kwa pyŏl kwa si)*. Chŏngŭmsa, 1948, 1955.

333

KIM KWANG-SŎP

Longing *(Tonggyŏng)*. Taedong insoeso, 1938.
Soul *(Maŭm)*. Chungang munhwa hyŏphoe, 1949.
Sunflowers *(Haebaragi)*. Chayu munhak hyŏphoe, 1957.
Sŏngbuktong Pigeons *(Sŏngbuktong pidŭlgi)*. Pŏmusa, 1969.
Response *(Panŭng)*. Munye ch'ulp'ansa, 1971.
Collected Works *(Kim Kwang-sŏp si chŏnjip)*. Ilchisa, 1974.
For his posthumous publications, see *Munhak sasang,* 69 (June 1978):267–285.

SŎ CHŎNG-JU

Flower Snake *(Hwasa chip)*. Namman sŏgo, 1938.
Cuckoo *(Kwich'okto)*. Sŏnmunsa, 1948.
Selected Poems *(Sŏ Chŏng-ju sisŏn)*. Chŏngŭmsa, 1956.
Silla Sketches *(Silla ch'o)*. Chŏngŭmsa, 1961.
Winter Sky *(Tongch'ŏn)*. Minjung sŏgwan, 1969.
Collected Works *(Sŏ Chŏng-ju munhak chŏnjip)*. 5 vols. Ilchisa, 1972. Vol. 1 contains poetry.
Myths of Chilmajae *(Chilmajae sinhwa)*. Ilchisa, 1975.
Poems of a Vagabond *(Ttŏdori ŭi si)*. Minŭmsa, 1976.

PAK TU-JIN

The Green Deer Anthology *(Ch'ŏngnok chip)*. Ŭryu munhwasa, 1946.
The Sun *(Hae)*. Ch'ŏngmansa, 1949.
Midday Prayer *(Odo)*. Yŏngung ch'ulp'ansa, 1953.
Selected Poems of Pak Tu-jin *(Pak Tu-jin sisŏn)*. Sŏngmun'gwan, 1956.
The Spider and the Constellation *(Kŏmi wa sŏngjwa)*. Taehan kidokkyohoeso, 1962.
The Human Jungle *(In'gan millim)*. Ilchogak, 1963.
White Wings *(Hayan nalgae)*. Hyangninsa, 1967.
High Mountain Plant *(Kosan singmul)*. Ilchisa, 1973.
The Acts of the Apostles *(Sado haengjŏn)*. Ilchisa, 1973.
Connected Traditions of Water-Washed Stones *(Susŏk yŏlchŏn)*. Ilchisa, 1973.
Connected Traditions of Water-Washed Stones Continued *(Sok susŏk yŏlchŏn)*. Ilchisa, 1976.

PAK MOGWŎL

The Green Deer Anthology *(Ch'ŏngnok chip)*. Ŭryu munhwasa, 1946.
Wild Peach Blossoms *(Sandohwa)*. Yŏngung ch'ulp'ansa, 1954.
Orchids and Others *(Nan kit'a)*. Sin'gu munhwasa, 1959.
Fair and Cloudy *(Ch'ŏngdam)*. Ilchogak, 1964.
Fallen Leaves of Kyŏngsang Province *(Kyŏngsangdo ŭi karangnip)*. Minjung sŏgwan, 1968.
Selected Works *(Pak Mogwŏl chasŏnjip)*. 10 vols. Samjungdang, 1973. Vols. 9 and 10 contain poetry.

One Hundred and One Poems *(Paegilp'yŏn ŭi si)*. Samjungdang, 1975.
Without Order *(Musun)*. Samjungdang, 1976.

KIM SU-YŎNG

The New City and the Chorus of Citizens *(Saeroun tosi wa simindŭrŭi hapch'ang)*.
   Tosi munhwasa, 1949.
The Game in the Moon *(Talnara ŭi changnan)*. Ch'unjosa, 1959.
The Huge Root: Selected Poems *(Kim Su-yŏng sisŏn: Kŏdaehan ppuri)*. Minŭmsa,
   1974.
Even If You Walked the Moon's Orbit *(Tarŭi haengno rŭl palbulchirado)*. Minŭm-
   sa, 1976.

KIM CH'UN-SU

Clouds and Roses *(Kurŭm kwa changmi)*. Haengmunsa, 1948.
The Swamp *(Nŭp)*. Yemunsa, 1949.
The Flag *(Ki)*. Pusan: Munyesa, 1951.
Sketches of the Flower *(Kkot ŭi somyo)*. Ch'ŏngjasa, 1958.
Death of a Girl in Budapest *(Budap'esut'u esŏŭi sonyŏ ŭi chugŭm)*. Ch'unjogak,
   1959.
The T'aryŏng Style and Other Poems *(T'aryŏngcho kit'a)*. Munhwa ch'ulp'ansa,
   1969.
Ch'ŏyong: Selected Poems *(Kim Ch'un-su sisŏn: Ch'ŏyong)*, Minŭmsa, 1974.
Southern Sky *(Namch'ŏn)*. Kŭnyŏk sŏjae, 1977.

SHIN TONG-YŎP

Asanyŏ. Munhaksa, 1963.
The Kŭm River *(Kŭmgang)*. Ŭryu munhwasa, 1967.
Collected Works *(Shin Tong-yŏp chŏnjip)*. Ch'angjak kwa pip'yŏngsa, 1975.

SHIN KYŎNG-NIM

Farmer's Dance *(Nongmu)*. Wŏlgan munhaksa, 1973.

HWANG TONG-GYU

One Fine Day *(Ŏttŏn kaein nal)*. Chungang munhwasa, 1961.
Sad Songs *(Piga)*. Ch'angusa, 1965.
Well-Tempered Clavier *(P'yŏnggyunnyul)*. Ch'angusa, 1968.
Well-Tempered Clavier, II. Hyŏndae munhaksa, 1972.
Snow Falls in the South: Selected Poems *(Hwang Tong-gyu sisŏn: Samname naeri-
   nŭn nun)*. Minŭmsa, 1974.
When I See a Wheel *(Nanŭn pak'wirŭl pomyŏn)*. Munhak kwa chisŏngsa, 1978.

CHŎNG HYŎN-JONG

The Dream of Things *(Samul ŭi kkum).* Minŭmsa, 1972.
The Festival of Pain: Selected Poems *(Chŏng Hyŏn-jong sisŏn: Kot'ong ŭi ch'uk-che).* Minŭmsa, 1974.
I'm a Star's Uncle *(Nanŭn pyŏl ajŏssi).* Munhak kwa chisŏngsa, 1978.

KIM CHI-HA

Yellow Earth *(Hwangt'o).* Hanŏl mun'go, 1970.
Japanese translations by Kyō Shun (Kang Sun) include Five Bandits, Yellow Earth, Groundless Rumors *(Gozoku, Kōdo, Higo)* (Tokyo: Aoki shoten, 1972), and Poetry of Kim Chi-ha *(Kin Shika shishū)* (Tokyo: Aoki shoten, 1974).
For English translations, see *Cry of the People and Other Poems* (Hayama: Autumn Press, 1974), and Chong Sun Kim and Shelly Killen, eds., *The Gold-Crowned Jesus and Other Writings* (Maryknoll: Orbis Books, 1978).

Translators

U-CH'ANG KIM. Born in 1936 in Korea, Kim studied at Seoul National University (B.A., 1958) and Cornell University (M.A., 1961) and received his Ph.D. from Harvard (1975) with his dissertation, "Politics, Poetry, and Culture: The Poetry of Wallace Stevens." He has taught English and American literature at Seoul National University, State University of New York at Buffalo, and Korea University, where he is professor of English. Editor of a prestigious literary quarterly in Korean, *World Literature,* he published a collection of critical essays, *The Poet in the Age of Need: Essays on Modern Korean Literature and Society* (Seoul, 1977). He is married and lives in Seoul with his wife and four children.

PETER H. LEE. Born in 1929 in Seoul, Korea, Lee was educated at Yale, Fribourg (Switzerland), Florence, Oxford, and Munich, where he received his Ph.D. (1958). Currently, he is professor of Korean and comparative literature at the University of Hawaii at Manoa. A Guggenheim Fellow, his recent publications include *Songs of Flying Dragons: A Critical Reading* (1975) and *Celebration of Continuity: Themes in Classic East Asian Poetry* (1979), both by Harvard University Press. A member of the International Council of the Translation Center at Columbia University, he also published an anthology of Korean poetry in English (1964; revised ed., 1974) and in German (1959).

DAVID R. MCCANN. Born in 1944, McCann was educated at Amherst and Harvard, where he received his Ph.D. with a thesis on "The Prosodic Structure of Pre-Modern Korean Verse" (1976). He spent several years in Korea as a Peace Corps volunteer (1966–1968) and Fulbright Scholar (1973–1974). His poems, translations, and critical essays have appeared in such journals as *Poetry, Modern Poetry in Translation,* and *Harvard Journal of Asiatic Studies.* He edited *Black Crane: An Anthology of Korean Literature* (Ithaca, 1977), and co-edited *Studies on Korea in Transition* (Honolulu, 1979). He is presently employed in the Office of University Development, Cornell University.

EDWARD D. ROCKSTEIN. Born in 1941, Rockstein first studied Korean while serving in the Army and later studied Korean and Japanese literature at Indiana University, followed by graduate work at Princeton. He acted in the Queen's Theatre Guild at Rutgers University and also with the Tin Barn Summer Theatre of Indiana University. After a year (1967–1968) in Korea on a Fulbright Fellowship, he taught Korean and East Asian civilization at Indiana University and at Colby College, Maine, from 1969 to 1975. Currently, he is a translator of Korean, Japanese, and Chinese for the U.S. government in Washington, D.C. He has published translations from Korean poetry.

SAMMY E. SOLBERG. Born in 1930 in Fertile, Minnesota, Solberg was reared and educated in and around Big Timber and Whitehall, Montana. He studied at Western Montana, the University of Washington, and Yonsei University in Seoul and received his Ph.D. from the University of Washington (1971) with a thesis on the poetry of Han Yong-un. He also did postdoctoral study on Asian American literature under a National Endowment for the Humanities Fellowship. He has published poems, translations, and critical essays in journals in Korea, Japan, the Philippines, and the United States, and has co-edited the "Korean Literature Issue" of *Literature East & West,* 14 (September 1970).

Index of Titles

Index of First Lines